**THE ROYAL COURT
THEATRE PRESENTS**

HOPE

By Jack Thorne

Hope was first performed at the
Royal Court Jerwood Theatre
Downstairs, Sloane Square, on
Wednesday 26th November 2014

D0233905

HOPE
BY JACK THORNE

CAST (in alphabetical order)

Sarwan **Rudi Dharmalingam**
Julie **Sharon Duncan-Brewster**
Laura **Jo Eastwood**
Gina **Christine Entwisle**
George **Tom Georgeson**
Hilary **Stella Gonet**
Mark **Paul Higgins**
Jake **Tommy Knight**
Lata/Alison **Nisha Nayar**

HOPE
BY JACK THORNE

Director **John Tiffany**
Designer **Tom Scutt**
Lighting Designer **Chahine Yavroyan**
Sound Designer **Carolyn Downing**
Composer & Musical Supervisor **Martin Lowe**
Assistant Director **Sandra Maturana**
Casting Director **Julia Horan CDG**
Production Manager **Tariq Rifaat**
Stage Manager **Laura Draper**
Deputy Stage Manager **Sarah Hellicar**
Assistant Stage Manager **Stuart Campbell**
Stage Management Work Placement **Ashley Lednor**
Costume Supervisor **Lucy Walshaw**
Set built by **Ridiculous Solutions Ltd**
Scenic work by **Luca Crestani**
Floor by **Footprint Scenery Ltd**
Curtains by **J. D. McDougall Ltd**

The Royal Court and Stage Management wish to thank the following for their help with this production:
Eleri Lloyd, James Turner Donnelly, Waterloo Library.

HOPE
THE COMPANY

Jack Thorne (Writer)

For the Royal Court: **Let the Right One In (& West End/Dundee Rep/National Theatre of Scotland/Marla Rubin Ltd).**

Other theatre includes: **Stuart: A Life Backwards (HighTide/Sheffield Theatres); The Borough (Punchdrunk/ Aldeburgh Festival); Mydidae (Drywrite/Soho/Trafalgar Studios); The Physicists (Donmar); Bunny (nabakov/International tour); 2nd May 1997 (& nabakov), Red Car Blue Car, Two Cigarettes, When You Cure Me (Bush); Greenland (National); Burying Your Brother in the Pavement (NT Connections); Stacy (Tron/Arcola/ Trafalgar Studios).**

Television includes: **Glue, The Fades, This is England '88, This is England '86, Cast-Offs, Skins, Shameless.**

Film includes: **War Book, The Scouting Book for Boys, A Long Way Down.**

Awards inlude: **BAFTA for Best Drama Series (The Fades), BAFTA for Best Mini-Series (This Is England '88), London Film Festival Best British Newcomer Award.**

Rudi Dharmalingam (Sarwan)

Theatre includes: **Worst Wedding Ever (Salisbury Playhouse); The Events (Young Vic/UK tour); The Seagull (Headlong/UK tour); Much Ado about Nothing (RSC/West End); You Can Still Make a Killing, England People Very Nice, Rafta Rafta (& UK tour), Tiger at the Gates, Playing With Fire (National); The English Game (Headlong); The Fastest Clock in the Universe (Naach); The History Boys (National/Broadway/ International tour); Tom's Midnight Garden (Unicorn); The Geri Project (Oldham Coliseum); Learning Styles (Impact); Anorak of Fire, The Tempest (Adelphi Studio, Salford); E to the Power 3, The Dispute (Robert Powell).**

Television includes: **Casualty, Doctor Who, Coronation Street, Hollyoaks, New Tricks, The Bill, Cutting It.**

Film includes: **Britz.**

Radio includes: **The Events, Tommies, Love Lies Sleeping for Boccaccio's Decameron, The Shape of Things.**

Carolyn Downing (Sound Designer)

For the Royal Court: **The Pass, Circle Mirror Transformation, The Low Road, The Witness, Our Private Life, Oxford Street, Alaska.**

Other theatre includes: **The House That Will Not Stand (Tricycle); Chimerica (Almeida/West End); Twelfth Night (Sheffield Crucible); Therese Raquin (Theatre Royal, Bath); Fathers & Sons, Lower Ninth, Dimetos, Absurdia (Donmar); Protest Song, Double Feature (National); Handbagged (Tricycle/West End); The Believers, Beautiful Burnout, Lovesong, Little Dogs (Frantic Assembly); King John, The Gods Weep, The Winter's Tale, Pericles, Days of Significance (RSC); Angels in America (Headlong); Blackta, After Miss Julie (Young Vic); Much Ado About Nothing, To Kill a Mockingbird, The Country Wife (Royal Exchange, Manchester); Blood Wedding (Almeida); Lulu, The Kreutzer Sonata, Vanya (Gate); The Water Engine (503); Stallerhof (Southwark); All My Sons (Broadway); Fanny och Alexander (Malmö Stadsteater); Amerika, Krieg der Bilder (Staatstheater, Mainz); Tre Kronor: Gustav III (Dramaten, Stockholm).**

Opera includes: **How The Whale Became (ROH); American Lulu (The Opera Group); After Dido (ENO).**

Exhibitions include: **Collider, Storybox: Constellation (Science Museum); From Street to Trench (Imperial War Museum North).**

Awards include: **Olivier for Best Sound Design (Chimerica).**

Sharon Duncan-Brewster (Julie)

For the Royal Court: **Crave (& Paines Plough), Yard Gal (& Clean Break), Babies.**

Other theatre includes: **The El Train (Hoxton Hall); A Few Man Fridays (Riverside/Cardboard Citizens); Yerma (Gate); The Swan, There is a War (National); Tiger Country (Hampstead); Detaining Justice, Seize the Day, Category B, Let There Be Love, Fabulation, Playboy of the West Indies (Tricycle); The Horse Marines (Theatre Royal, Plymouth); The Bacchae (National Theatre of Scotland); Black Crows (Clean Break/Arcola); The Magic Carpet (Lyric, Hammersmith); Blues for Mr Charlie (Talawa/Tricycle/New Wolsey, Ipswich); Dirty Butterfly (Soho); Peep Show (Frantic Assembly/Drum, Plymouth/Lyric, Hammersmith); Keepers (Hampstead); So Special (Royal Exchange, Manchester); The No Boys Cricket Club (Theatre Royal, Stratford East).**

Television includes: **Cucumber, Top Boy, Doctor Who, EastEnders, Bad Girls, Doctors, Shoot the Messenger, Waking the Dead, Holby City, Baby Father, The Mimic, The Bible.**

Jo Eastwood (Laura)

Theatre includes: **The Yellow Wallpaper (& UK tour), Notre Dame de Paris (& European tour), Frankie & Johnnie (Strathcona).**

Television Includes: **Frankie, Casualty, EastEnders, The Spastic King, Kingdom.**

Film Includes: **Hellboy, English Goodbye, Sweetheart.**

Radio includes: **Novavox.**

Christine Entwisle (Gina)

For the Royal Court: **Primetime, Narrative, The Wonderful World of Dissocia (& Tron/Drum, Plymouth/ Edinburgh International Festival/ tour).**

Other theatre includes: **Billy the Girl (Clean Break/Soho); Titus (Theory of Everything); As You Like It, The Comedy of Errors, Romeo & Juliet, Silence, The Drunks, Morte D'Athur (RSC); Six Characters in Search of an Author (Gielgud/Headlong/Chichester Festival); Half Life (National Theatre of Scotland); C'est Vauxhall! (Duckie/ Barbican); Genetics for Blondes (Soho); The Wedding (Southwark Playhouse/National tour); Vassa**

(Almeida/The Albery); A Family Affair (Clwyd); Wonderhorse (Edinburgh International Festival/ICA/BAC); Edward Gant's Amazing Feats of Loneliness (Theatre Royal, Plymouth/ Headlong); I Am Dandy (Purcell Rooms/ BAC); Ubu Kunst, Missing Jesus (Young Vic); Paper Walls (Scarlet/Assembly Rooms/Purcell Rooms); Fine (Young Vic/Edinburgh International Festival); People Shows 100–103 (International tour).

Television includes: **Attachments, Holby City, Mothers & Daughters, At Dawning, A&E, Where the Heart Is, Dalziel & Pascoe, Storm Damage, Deeper Still.**

Radio includes: **Heredity.**

Awards include: **Tron Award for Best Actress, Critics' Award for Theatre in Scotland for Best Female Performance (The Wonderful World Of Dissocia).**

Tom Georgeson (George)

For the Royal Court: **Incomplete & Random Acts of Kindness.**

Other theatre includes: **Longing, Glass Eels (Hampstead); Judgement Day, Lulu (Almeida); When We Are Married (West Yorkshire Playhouse/Liverpool Playhouse); Mother Courage (ETT); The Kindness of Strangers (Everyman, Liverpool); The Seagull (Edinburgh International Festival); Frozen, The Good Hope (National); Frozen (Birmingham Rep); Treasure Island (Lyric, Hammersmith); Dealer's Choice (National/West End); King Baby (RSC); Sixteen Words for Water (Old Red Lion); Across the Ferry, The Marshalling Yard (Bush).**

Television includes: **New Tricks, Frankie, Casualty, Henry IV (Parts 1 &2), Henry V, The Way to Go, Law & Order, Doctors, Justice, The Suspicions of Mr Whicher, The Crimson Petal & the White, Holby City, Shameless, Ashes to Ashes, Our Mutual Friends, Hancock & Joan, The Inspector Lynley Mysteries, English Harem, Under the Greenwood Tree, Midsomer Murders, Bleak House, Waking the Dead, Poirot, Foyle's War, Clocking Off, Liverpool One, Silent Witness, Dalziel & Pascoe, A Touch of Frost, Wuthering Heights, Between the Lines, G.B.H., The Manageress, Boys from the Blackstuff.**

Film includes: **Electricity, The Real Life of Angel Deverell, Notes on a Scandal,**

Irish Jam, Man Dancin', The Virgin of Liverpool, Morality Play, Swing, Land Girls, Downtime, Fairytale: A True Story, Fierce Creatures, A Fish Called Wanda, No Surrender Kim.

Stella Gonet (Hilary)

For the Royal Court: The Slab Boys Trilogy (& Traverse).

Other theatre includes: Handbagged (Tricycle/West End); Before the Party (Almeida); Top Girls (Chichester Festival/West End); The Memory of Water, Cyrano De Bergerac (West End); Women, Power & Politics (Tricycle); Hilda (Hampstead); Skylight (National/West End); Measure for Measure, After Easter, A Midsummer Night's Dream, Divine Gossip, Three Sisters, The Revenger's Tragedy, The Jew of Malta, Fashion, Heresies, The Archbishop's Ceiling (RSC); Racing Demon, The Shaughraun, The Voysey Inheritance, Hamlet, True Dare Kiss, Command or Promise (National); Points of Departure (Traverse/tour); Trafford Tanzi (Mermaid).

Television includes: Siblings, Father Brown, Hacks, Lewis, Mo, Holby City, Rebus, Roman Mysteries, Persuasion, Dalziel & Pascoe, Mysterious Murders, Where the Heart Is, Murder in Suburbia, Taggart, The Inspector Lynley Mysteries, Foyle's War, Midsomer Murders, The Secret, Verdict, Supply & Demand, The Crow Road, Trip Trap, House of Eliot, The Advocates, The Common Pursuit, Heading Home, The Bill, Down Where the Buffalo Go, Casualty, The Shutter Falls, To Have & To Hold.

Film includes: How I Live Now, Dirty Bomb, Nicholas Nickleby, Stalin, For Queen & Country.

Radio includes: The Piano, Women in Love, Before I Go to Sleep, Skylight, Book of the Week, Book at Bedtime.

Awards include: Royal Television Society Award for Best Actress (Trip Trap).

Paul Higgins (Mark)

For the Royal Court: Night Songs, American Bagpipe, The Conquest of the South Pole, A Wholly Healthy Glasgow.

Other theatre includes: Children of the Sun, Paul, The White Guard, An Enemy of the People, The Hare Trilogy (National); King Lear (Citizens); Luise Miller, The Cosmonaut's Last Message (Donmar); Black Watch (National Theatre of Scotland); Damascus (Traverse/Tricycle/Middle East tour); The Tempest (Tron); Macbeth, Conversations After A Burial (Almeida); Measure for Measure (RSC); The Golden Ass, A Midsummer Night's Dream (Globe); Buried Alive (Hampstead); Macbeth (ETT/Lyric, Hammersmith); The Slab Boys Trilogy (Young Vic).

Television includes: Utopia, Line of Duty, The Thick of It, Case Histories, Vera, The Last Enemy, New Town, Silent Witness, No Holds Bard, Low Winter Sun, Murder, Beating Jesus, Staying Alive, Dr Finlay, Tumbledown, A Very Peculiar Practice, A Wholly Healthy Glasgow, The Negotiator.

Film Includes: Couple in a Hole, In the Loop, Red Road, Complicity, Bedrooms & Hallways.

Tommy Knight (Jake)

Theatre includes: Macbeth (RSC); The Snowman (Sadler's Wells); Chitty Chitty Bang Bang, Medea (West End).

Television includes: Glue, Waterloo Road, Dr Who, The Sarah Jane Adventures, The Bill, Sorted, The Impressionists, Casualty.

Film includes: Stitches.

Martin Lowe (Composer & Musical Supervisor)

As Musical Director, theatre includes: Once, Loserville, The Full Monty, Once on This Island (West End); Jedermann (Salzburg Festival); The Light Princess, Nation, Caroline or Change, Once in a Lifetime, A Funny Thing Happened on the Way to the Forum (National); Once (New York Theatre Workshop); War Horse (National/West End); The Wolves in the Wall (National Theatre of Scotland/Improbable); Jerry Springer the Opera (National/West End/BAC/Assembly Rooms); Mamma Mia! (West End/International tour); Is There Life After High School? (Bridewell); Cats (West End/UK tour); Pal Joey, Last Train to Berlin (Minerva); Maddie (Salisbury Playhouse); Definitely Doris (King's Head); Closer Than Ever (Jermyn Street).

As Musical Associate, theatre includes: Les Misérables, Moby Dick, Which Witch

(West End); Nine (Royal Festival Hall); Just So (Tricycle).

As Composer, theatre includes: **The Misanthrope, The Secret Rapture, Hysteria (Minerva); The Blue Room (Minerva/West End); Lettice & Lovage (Theatre Royal, Bath/UK tour).**

As Composer, radio Includes: **Into Exile, Dear Exile.**

Sandra Maturana (Assistant Director)

As Assistant Director, theatre includes: **My Dad's a Birdman (Young Vic); Seven Angels (The Opera Group/ROH/tour); The Mouse & His Child (RSC).**

As Director, theatre includes: **Hamlyn, Resolutions (The Space); Yerma (RSC Studio); A Date with Doris (Riverside); Building Walls (503); Alice's Shadow (Edinburgh International Festival/Tara Arts); The Love of Don Perlimplin, 00:13 (Albany); Borderlands (Ovalhouse); A Spatial Discovery (BAC); Quixote (HighTide Studio); Dreams of the Orient (Fairfield Hall).**

As Movement Director, theatre includes: **The Government Inspector (Parallel Production/Young Vic); Socrates & His Clouds (Jermyn Street); Venus/Mars (Bush); Frankenstein: The Opera (The Space).**

Nisha Nayar (Lata/Alison)

Theatre includes: **Sisters (Crucible, Sheffield); Our Own Kind (Bush); The Optimist's Daughter (Finborough); Sanctuary (Riverside).**

Television includes: **Law & Order, Count Arthur Strong, Casualty, The Bill, Cracker, Rose & Maloney, Doctor Who, Tracy Beaker, Holby City, Sirens, Big Bad World, Out of Hours, Holding On, Underground, The Buddha of Suburbia, True Love, Cardiac Arrest, Full Stretch, Medics, London Bridge, Cone Zone, Bhangra Girls.**

Film includes: **In America, The Principles of Lust, The Darkest Light, Different for Girls, Sixth Happiness, Bhaji on the Beach.**

Radio includes: **Inquest, Resolutions, We Are a Muslim, Please, Have Your Cake, Seymour the Fractal Cat, Selfless, Rescue Me, Brave Faces, Me & Billie Marker, The Bandit Queen, Midnight Musing, Hardly Touching, Orlando,**

Women of the Dust, The Brahmin & the Lady, The Ramayana, Skeleton, Grease Monkeys, Girlies, Up & Running, Mera Das, The Jungle Book, Crinklies, Kiss Me Quick, We Are Mesquakie, Voices on the Wind, My Enemy, My Friend, Girlfriends, The Burning Glass, The Goondas of Gopingar, Have Your Say, Westway, Resolutions, Mixed Blood, Silver Street, The Heart & Heaven, Stars.

Tom Scutt (Designer)

For the Royal Court: **Constellations (& West End), The Djinns of Eidgah, The Ritual Slaughter of Gorge Mastromas, No Quarter, Remembrance Day.**

Other theatre includes: **East is East (Trafalgar Studios); King Charles III (& Almeida), Absent Friends (West End); Medea, 13 (National); Mr Burns; King Lear; Through A Glass Darkly (Almeida); The Weir (Donmar/West End); A Number (Nuffield, Sheffield); South Downs/The Browning Version (West End/Chichester Festival); The Life of Galileo (RSC/Birmingham Rep/UK tour); Romeo & Juliet, The Merchant of Venice (RSC); A Midsummer Night's Dream, Edward Gant's Amazing Feats of Loneliness (Theatre Royal, Plymouth/ Headlong); The Lion, the Witch & the Wardrobe (Kensington Gardens); Hamlet (Sheffield Theatres); Mogadishu (Royal Exchange, Manchester/ Lyric, Hammersmith); Cinderella, Jack & the Beanstalk, Aladdin, Dick Whittington (Lyric, Hammersmith); Vanya, Unbroken, The Internationalist (Gate); Bay (Young Vic); The Merchant of Venice (Octagon, Bolton); Metropolis (Theatre Royal, Bath).**

Opera includes: **How The Whale Became (ROH); Wozzeck (as Set Designer) (ENO); The Flying Dutchman (Scottish Opera); Rigoletto (Opera Holland Park).**

Awards include: **The Linbury Biennial Prize for Stage Design, The Jocelyn Herbert Award, WhatsOnStage Award for Best Set Designer (Constellations; The Lion, the Witch & the Wardrobe).**

Tom is Associate Designer for the Nuffield Theatre.

John Tiffany (Director)

For the Royal Court: **The Pass, Let the Right One In (& West End/Dundee Rep/ National Theatre of Scotland/Marla Rubin Ltd).**

Other theatre includes: **The Ambassador (BAM, New York); Macbeth, Enquirer (co-director), The Missing, Peter Pan, The House of Bernarda Alba, Transform Caithness: Hunter, Be Near Me, Nobody Will Ever Forgive Us, The Bacchae, Black Watch, Elizabeth Gordon Quinn, Home: Glasgow (National Theatre of Scotland); Once (West End/Broadway/New York Theatre Workshop); The Glass Menagerie (Broadway/American Repertory); Jerusalem (West Yorkshire Playhouse); Las Chicas de Tres Y Media Floppies (Granero, Mexico City); If Destroyed True (& Dundee Rep), Mercury Fur, The Straits, Helmet (Paines Plough); Gagarin Way, Abandonment, Among Unbroken Hearts, Passing Places (Traverse).**

Awards include: **Tony, Obie & Drama Desk Awards (Once), Olivier Award for Best Director, Critics' Circle Award for Best Director, South Bank Show Award (Black Watch).**

John is an Associate Director at the Royal Court. From 2010 to 2011, he was a Radcliffe Fellow at Harvard University.

Chahine Yavroyan (Lighting Designer)

For the Royal Court: **Khandan (Family) (& Birmingham Rep), The Pass, Let the Right One In, Narrative, Get Santa, Wig Out!, Relocated, The Lying Kind, Almost Nothing, At the Table, Bazaar, Another Wasted Year.**

Other theatre includes: **King Lear, The House, Major Barbara (Abbey); A Soldier in Every Son, Measure for Measure, Marat/Sade, Dunsinane (& National Theatre of Scotland), God in Ruins, Little Eagles (RSC); Farewell, Half a Glass of Water (Field Day); Uncle Vanya (Minerva); The Lady from the Sea, The Comedy of Errors, Three Sisters (Royal Exchange, Manchester); Scorched (Old Vic Tunnels); FuenteOvejuna, Punishment Without Revenge, Dr Faustus (Madrid); Elizabeth Gordon Quinn, Caledonia, Realism, The Wonderful World of Dissocia (National Theatre of Scotland); Orphans, Dallas Sweetman, Long Time Dead (Paines Plough); Dr Marigold & Mr Chops (Riverside Studios); Jane Eyre, Someone Who'll Watch Over Me (Perth); Il Tempo del Postino (Manchester International Festival); How to Live (Barbican).**

Dance includes: **Jasmin Vardimon Dance,**

Bock & Vincenzi, Frauke Requardt, Colin Poole, CanDoCo, Ricochet, Rosemary Lee, Arthur Pita.

Music work includes: **XX Scharnhorst (HMS Belfast); Sevastopol, Home (ROH2); Plague Songs (Barbican); Dalston Songs (ROH2); The Death of Klinghoffer (Scottish Opera); Jocelyn Pook Ensemble, Diamanda Galas (International).**

Site specific work includes: **Paradise Lost (Archway Tower); Focal Point (Rochester Harbour); Enchanted Parks (Newcastle); Dreams of a Winter Night (Belsay Hall); Deep End (Marshall St Baths); Ghost Sonata (Sefton Park, Palmhouse).**

UNTIL MAY 2015

"All of these plays are about revolutions – big and small acts of resistance. They are provocative, diverse and timely. They are great stories, inventively told and demanding that we consider a better future"

Vicky Featherstone
Artistic Director

JERWOOD THEATRE
UPSTAIRS

7 – 31 Jan
Liberian Girl
By Diana Nneka Atuona

This Alfred Fagon award-winning play tells one teenage girl's story of survival.

12 Feb – 14 Mar
Fireworks
by Dalia Taha

This new Palestinian play gives us a new way of seeing how war fractures childhood.

JERWOOD THEATRE
DOWNSTAIRS

4 Feb – 21 Mar
How To Hold Your Breath
By Zinnie Harris

An epic look at the true cost of principles and how we live now.

7 Apr – 31 May
Roald Dahl's
The Twits
By Enda Walsh

Mischievously adapted from one of the world's most loved books, Enda Walsh turns the The Twits upside down.

020 7565 5000 (no booking fee)
royalcourttheatre.com

Follow us 🐦 royalcourt 📘 royalcourttheatre
Royal Court Theatre Sloane Square London, SW1W 8AS

THE ROYAL COURT THEATRE

The Royal Court Theatre is the writers' theatre. It is the leading force in world theatre for energetically cultivating writers – undiscovered, new, and established.

Through the writers the Royal Court is at the forefront of creating restless, alert, provocative theatre about now, inspiring audiences and influencing future writers. Through the writers the Royal Court strives to constantly reinvent the theatre ecology, creating theatre for everyone.

We invite and enable conversation and debate, allowing writers and their ideas to reach and resonate beyond the stage, and the public to share in the thinking.

Over 120,000 people visit the Royal Court in Sloane Square, London, each year and many thousands more see our work elsewhere through transfers to the West End and New York, national and international tours, residencies across London and site-specific work.

The Royal Court's extensive development activity encompasses a diverse range of writers and artists and includes an ongoing programme of writers' attachments, readings, workshops and playwriting groups. Twenty years of pioneering work around the world means the Royal Court has relationships with writers on every continent.

The Royal Court opens its doors to radical thinking and provocative discussion, and to the unheard voices and free thinkers that, through their writing, change our way of seeing.

Within the past sixty years, John Osborne, Arnold Wesker and Howard Brenton have all started their careers at the Court. Many others, including Caryl Churchill, Mark Ravenhill and Sarah Kane have followed. More recently, the theatre has found and fostered new writers such as Polly Stenham, Mike Bartlett, Bola Agbaje, Nick Payne and Rachel De-lahay and produced many iconic plays from Laura Wade's **Posh** to Bruce Norris' **Clybourne Park** and Jez Butterworth's **Jerusalem**. Royal Court plays from every decade are now performed on stage and taught in classrooms across the globe.

It is because of this commitment to the writer that we believe there is no more important theatre in the world than the Royal Court.

Supported using public funding by

ARTS COUNCIL ENGLAND

ROYAL COURT SUPPORTERS

The Royal Court has significant and longstanding relationships with many organisations and individuals who provide vital support. It is this support that makes possible its unique playwriting and audience development programmes.

Coutts supports Innovation at the Royal Court. The Genesis Foundation supports the Royal Court's work with International Playwrights. Alix Partners support The Big Idea at the Royal Court.
The Jerwood Charitable Foundation supports emerging writers through the Jerwood New Playwrights series. The Pinter Commission is given annually by his widow, Lady Antonia Fraser, to support a new commission at the Royal Court.

PUBLIC FUNDING

Arts Council England, London
British Council

CHARITABLE DONATIONS

The Austin & Hope Pilkington
  Charitable Trust
Martin Bowley Charitable Trust
Cowley Charitable Trust
The Dorset Foundation
The Eranda Foundation
Genesis Foundation
The Golden Bottle Trust
The Haberdashers' Company
The Idlewild Trust

Roderick & Elizabeth Jack
Jerwood Charitable Foundation
Marina Kleinwort Trust
The Andrew Lloyd Webber Foundation
John Lyon's Charity
Clare McIntyre's Bursary
The Andrew W. Mellon Foundation
The David & Elaine Potter Foundation
Rose Foundation
Royal Victoria Hall Foundation
The Sackler Trust
The Sobell Foundation
John Thaw Foundation
The Vandervell Foundation
Sir Siegmund Warburg's Voluntary Settlement
The Garfield Weston Foundation
The Wolfson Foundation

CORPORATE SUPPORTERS & SPONSORS

AKA
Alix Partners
Aqua Financial Solutions Ltd
Bloomberg
Colbert
Coutts
Fever-Tree
Gedye & Sons
MAC

BUSINESS ASSOCIATES, MEMBERS & BENEFACTORS

Annoushka
Auerbach & Steele Opticians
Byfield Consultancy
Capital MSL
Cream
Heal's
Lazard
Salamanca Group
Vanity Fair

DEVELOPMENT ADVOCATES

Elizabeth Bandeen
Anthony Burton CBE
Piers Butler
Sindy Caplan
Sarah Chappatte
Cas Donald (Vice Chair)
Celeste Fenichel
Piers Gibson
Emma Marsh (Chair)
Deborah Shaw
  (Vice Chair)
Tom Siebens
Sian Westerman

Innovation partner

Supported using public funding by
ARTS COUNCIL ENGLAND

EMPLOYEES
THE ROYAL COURT & ENGLISH STAGE COMPANY

The Royal Court has been on the cutting edge of new drama for more than 50 years. Thanks to our members, we are able to undertake the vital support of writers and the development of their plays – work which is the lifeblood of the theatre.

In acknowledgement of their support, members are invited to venture beyond the stage door to share in the energy and creativity of Royal Court productions.

Please join us as a member to celebrate our shared ambition whilst helping to ensure our ongoing success.

We can't do it without you.

royalcourttheatre.com

BECOME A MEMBER

To join as a Royal Court member from £250 a year, please contact

Anna Sampson, Development Manager
annasampson@royalcourttheatre.com
020 7565 5049

HOPE

Jack Thorne

For Fiona Green

'Laws are like sausages. It is better not to see them being made.'

Otto von Bismarck

4

Central Characters

MARK, *mid- to late forties*
JULIE, *early thirties*
HILARY, *early fifties*
GINA, *mid- to late forties*
LAURA, *mid-thirties*
SARWAN, *mid-thirties*
LATA, *late thirties*
JAKE, *fifteen*
GEORGE, *mid-seventies*
ALISON, *mid-thirties*

Other parts played by members of the company.

The action is set predominantly in and around a 1920s-era council office. The sort of place that has beautiful lead-lined glass windows and ugly 1970s furniture.

This text went to press before the end of rehearsals and so may differ slightly from the play as performed.

Prologue

LAURA. Hello.

Merry Christmas.

My grandmother always told me that if I was a good girl
Father Christmas would come.

My grandfather told me she was lying.

I thought it was safer to be a good girl – in case she wasn't.
Lying.

I told her I was a good girl.

She asked me what I thought a good girl was.

And I just laughed.

She liked that.

Did I say already Merry Christmas?

I don't believe in Father Christmas any more.

I stopped believing – well, I won't tell you when…

This is –

This is the story of my town.

This is the story of good men – and women – good – people.

This is the story of my year in politics.

ACT ONE

Scene One

It's night. MARK*'s flat. Which is a nice-enough flat.*

MARK. The council is required to have £64 million of savings
by 2017.

This year this means losing £22 million from our projected
budget.

Now this is all to be expected, we live in an age of cuts after
all. Cost savings have been a priority for this Council for the
last few years and the main focus of our activity. But that
means the cost savings are no longer something we're afraid
of – we intend to attack this head-on. This Council is one
that isn't afraid to make the hard decisions. Hard and right.

He makes a face to himself.

This Council is one that isn't afraid to make the hard
decisions. As long as they're also the right decisions. We're
currently re-examining every single cost – every single entry
on our books to find where the savings can come with the
least damage to front-line services.

Thank you – any questions.

JULIE. I don't understand – in an age of cuts – I thought
austerity measures were largely being phased out now – that
Britain is booming.

MARK. I can't speak for the country – I can speak for this
Council. And I can tell you that in this part of the world –
we're not booming – and the Government changes I already
outlined have meant – austerity remains more or less entirely
our focus.

JULIE. But if it has – been your focus – Councillor – then why
weren't these cuts better anticipated? Why do you need to

re-examine anything? Surely you should have decided
months – years ago – where the axe must fall?

MARK. They were – anticipated – anticipated? Anticipated, but
not quite at this level.

We previously projected our cuts at £14.1 million. But
Government cuts in the Early Intervention Grant used to
fund early-years services and the Government's intention to
create a contingency fund from our pot – to cover possible
future deficits have created what we believe to be
approximately £7.9 million in additional savings. Taking us
to £22 million. £22 million we need to save. Is that? Did I
just sound really proud of myself for doing some mental
arithmetic?

JULIE. It's fine. Smile.

MARK *smiles.*

Okay. On to specific areas, after three years of cuts it's likely
you're going to have to hunt quite hard for these savings…
Where are these spending cuts likely to hit?

MARK. Our aim is to make them as painless as possible. To
make efficiency savings rather than cut services, but
undoubtedly hard decisions will have to be made…

JULIE. Will for instance rubbish collection…

MARK. I could go through your list with you – but the truth is,
key decisions have yet to be made. All I can say is that these
decisions will be taken with the utmost care and… I'm
fucking this up, aren't I?

JULIE. Fundamentally, why, in a time –

MARK. I shouldn't have interrupted you…

JULIE. Interruptions are fine.

Deputy Leader, surely you can give us some indication on
where the cuts will fall…

MARK. The Government cuts and the resultant budgetary
savings –

JULIE. Breathe.

MARK. The Government cuts and the –

JULIE. Honestly, Mark, breathe…

MARK. The Government cuts – breathe – and the resultant budget – breathe – ary – savings – breathe –

JULIE. Now you're sounding like Malcolm Rifkind.

MARK. – are going to fall harder on us than anyone else. I can't lie to you about that. We're a working-class town, and the sectors which have kept us in employment are both in long-term decline and have yet to emerge from their short-term dip, and so our dependence on central government support has bitten us harder than it might of other more affluent towns.

JULIE. That's good. That's great.

MARK. But our weaknesses are also our strengths.

As a working-class town we're not afraid… Am I just repeating myself?

JULIE. You're doing fine. Repeating yourself is good.

MARK. It feels like I'm talking utter bollocks.

JULIE. The working-class thing. Not being afraid. It was nice.

MARK. You sure?

JULIE. Start again.

From the beginning. Councillor, how does it feel to be presiding over the worst cuts in the history of this town? Cuts that just seem to continue on year after year?

MARK. The Council is required to have £64 million of savings by 2017. This year this means losing £22 million from our projected budget. We live in the age of cuts. To ignore the cuts is to ignore… What did I say…?

JULIE. You shouldn't know this all by rote. It's good to vary…

MARK. We live in the age of cuts.

Shit.

We live in an age of cuts.

JULIE. We live in an age of cunts.

MARK. We live in an age of cunts. To ignore the cunts is to ignore reality.

JULIE *smiles*.

JULIE. It's nice. It works.

MARK. We live in the age of cutting cunts. To cut a cunt you just insert your knife and pull.

JULIE *looks at* MARK.

Too much?

JULIE. Vaginal mutilation might not go down so well with the women's vote.

MARK. No.

JULIE. Oh, and your flies are open.

He checks. He exclaims.

MARK. This sodding suit. It just does it. Automatically.

JULIE. Your flies just open... automatically...

MARK. Yes.

JULIE. Automatically?

MARK. Yes. Yes. Should I – do we do it again?

They look at each other a moment more.

I do think – I do think this is going to be a shit time – and I have a truly shit job – but I do think we can be the – I do think we can make the best of it better than anyone else can.

JULIE. And that's why it's worth doing the shit job? You should say that.

MARK. I mean that.

JULIE *smiles*.

ACT TWO

Scene One

MARK. You'd be amazed what matters.

> Taps at graves matter. And taxi licensing. Now that's important.

> Deciding who'll have the licence to pick your town's teenage girls up at night.

SARWAN. Allotments. I probably get more letters about allotments…

JULIE. Traffic lights. Speed cameras. Speed bumps.

SARWAN. I had one man practically hang himself in front of me because we increased our allotment rates from £25 to £30 a year.

> He kept trying to tell me about the cost of compost.

JULIE. Speed bumps I think probably account for about forty per cent of my correspondence.

> Those that want them removed.

LATA. Welfare issues. Credit issues. The amount of residents who complain to me about their credit-card companies… I explain I can't help with that. I send them to the Citizens Advice Bureau.

JULIE. Those that want them kept. Those who want more. Those who want less.

LATA. I get a little jingle in my head whenever I say 'Citizens Advice Bureau'.

HILARY. Council tax.

MARK. Parking charges – not so steep that people park on residential streets, not so low that the yield for the Council isn't so much.

That matters. Parking revenue is hugely important.

LATA (*sings*). Citizens Advice Bureau.

HILARY. Benefits. Tax.

SARWAN. One man asked me in all sincerity whether I could bring back the eight-track tape deck.

HILARY. You do get people who think you are the Government.

SARWAN. Some people who think you are God.

LATA (*sings*). Citizens Advice Bureau.

HILARY. But most understand the limits of your job.

MARK. The truth is...

   It all matters.

   The achievements are small but plentiful.

   Because it all matters.

HILARY. We matter.

SARWAN. And we like the fact we do.

Scene Two

The corridor of a day centre for adults with learning difficulties.

HILARY. I don't have long...

GINA. We don't need long.

HILARY. A favour. Please. Before we go in. Just don't let me talk to anyone who'll – embarrass me.

GINA. They're not embarrassing, Hilary. They're disabled.

   No one here will embarrass you.

HILARY. I'm here because you asked me.

And because you're an old friend. Well, Mark is a friend and...

GINA. Everyone's excited at the visit from the Leader of the Council.

It's a day-centre bake-off. All you need to do is judge the winner. And then scoot.

HILARY *looks at her.*

HILARY. One time. One woman insisted on showing me her bra. Fine in a social context. In a public context, a pain in the arse. With the press here, you know?

GINA. It's just a photographer from the local paper, Hilary. Surely you're used to this sort of thing?

HILARY. Yes. Yes. Do you have a mint?

GINA. No.

HILARY. I think my breath smells.

GINA. I don't think it does.

HILARY. Can I breathe on you?

GINA. Okay.

HILARY *breathes in* GINA's *face.*

HILARY. Okay?

GINA. Eggs for breakfast?

HILARY. Yes. Is it bad?

GINA. Only when you breathe in someone's face. Shall we go in?

HILARY. Yes. Sorry. I get nervous before all these things.

GINA. Hil. You would tell me, wouldn't you?

If we were getting cut...

HILARY. Of course I'd tell you.

GINA. Because I've been asking you here for more than a few years so if... you're here just so you can say you visited before cutting...

HILARY. No. No.

Now, let's see these cakes!

Scene Three

Council corridor.

SARWAN. You're on my bench.

JULIE. I'm on 'a' bench.

SARWAN. What are you in for?

JULIE. Road-signage-graffiti-snitch-line thing we're trying to set up. And then I've got Healthier Together. Health Series Review. Joint HOSC.

SARWAN. Hosc? I'm not sure I've –

JULIE. Health Overview Scrutiny Committee. Say it fast and it almost sounds magic. What are you in for?

SARWAN. RCC. Railways Consultative Committee. Councillor Phillip Samson –

JULIE (*impression*). Councillor Philip Samson.

SARWAN. – has just explained to me the difference between the Stephenson gauge and the Brunel gauge. I'm on a pee break. I've got – (*Checks his watch.*) five minutes before they assume I have kidney stones.

SARWAN *sits beside her and offers her a new Snickers from his pocket.*

Snickers?

JULIE. You have one spare?

SARWAN. Always.

And I'm offering my spare – to you.

JULIE. Do you have any idea what that shit does to your arteries?

SARWAN. Snickers calm me.

JULIE. Learn yoga.

SARWAN. You do know I'm Indian?

JULIE. Yeah. So…

SARWAN. Yoga is what we do.

JULIE. You don't.

SARWAN. Not literally, no. But in my mind. I'm a bit of a guru.

He pulls a few moves.

JULIE. That's kung fu.

SARWAN. Not in India it's not.

SARWAN *sits beside* JULIE. *He eats the chocolate off his Snickers. She looks at him and frowns. He starts to eat the Snickers more normally.*

So – tonight feels like a significant moment.

JULIE. The Councillor is referring to the meeting to which we've not been invited to?

SARWAN. He is. Big night.

JULIE. The biggest.

SARWAN. Yeah. My wedding night might feature slightly higher…

JULIE. My graduation.

SARWAN. The birth of my firstborn…

JULIE. The death of my mother…

SARWAN. I'm sorry.

JULIE. Fifteen years ago. Carry on… I'm enjoying the one-upmanship…

SARWAN. My first kiss was a pretty big day.

JULIE. Thank you for not saying first wank.

SARWAN. I'm a romantic.

He looks at her. She smiles.

How do you rate your chances of ever making it? The Budget Steering Group?

JULIE. Poor. You?

SARWAN. Eventually: good. Hilary seems to support me despite herself. And Lata's vulnerable. And brown needs to be replaced by brown.

JULIE. What am I – pink?

SARWAN. And she's not a Muzzie like me. And Muzzies score mega-top-trump points. In this area.

JULIE. And you'd want to be on it?

SARWAN. What?

JULIE. If you won. You'd want to be on it?

SARWAN. Yes. Yes. I think so. I mean, at least it'd be interesting.

Wouldn't you?

JULIE. Yes. I think so too.

It's just…

Three years in…

SARWAN. You feel like the only job the Budget Steering Group has is to navigate us into the iceberg?

You may be right.

Scene Four

A Budget Steering Group meeting. In a small office with a round table.

HILARY. Right.

MARK. So, here we go again…

HILARY. Ha. Yes. So… For ease of…

What I've done is, I've gone through the list, all the projects and I've actually – I've drawn up – as a discussion document – what I would cut – just as a way of –

LATA. Quantifying. Possible… Quantifying possibilities.

HILARY. And Lata has been a huge help in working out – I don't want you to see this as a – it's just me trying to be helpful. As helpful as I might be. But nothing is – far from it – nothing is off the discussion plate.

MARK. Okay. That makes sense.

HILARY. We're still looking to increase council tax by one-point-nine per cent across the board – the largest increase we can have without triggering a referendum.

LATA. Which we would lose.

HILARY. And which they kindly put into our constitutions. For this we will get a yield of about £330,000. Which is…

LATA. A dent in the ocean.

HILARY. Dent?

MARK. So we need to cut our way to a solution.

HILARY. Yes. We do.

HILARY *smiles.*

Shall we start from the top then?

LATA. City farm…

HILARY *reads the list.*

HILARY. Proposed gone.

MARK. I didn't even know we paid for that.

HILARY. Should have gone three years ago. Councillor Ali liked the ponies.

LATA. Swimming pool.

MARK. Haven't they only just finished their extension works?

HILARY. According to this, it costs £120,000 a year upkeep. I've proposed halving their budget.

MARK. Which would result in...?

LATA. We'd lose some classes, aqua aerobics will take quite a hit, and we may need to restrict opening hours...

HILARY. Done. Surely. That's an easy one. We've also got £50,000 off street lighting...

MARK. How?

A map is slid across the table. MARK *studies it.*

LATA. Half-hour later and earlier in the summer months.

We are making the days longer.

MARK. And we're cutting it entirely by the marsh and on the roads around Longbridge.

LATA. We're allocating it more precisely.

MARK. There were how many rapes in Longbridge in the last five years? Five? Six?

LATA. Three. Which is why we launched a rape-alarm initiative there last year. The roads are barely used at night. None of the victims were seized from the street.

MARK. They can be now.

HILARY. Okay. So this seems to require further discussion. Shall we return to it later? I'll mark it with a star.

LATA. Public toilets are down as a maybe.

HILARY. Yes. Where I wasn't sure I just put maybe.

LATA. I'd make them a definite. A lot of other councils cut them last year. I just use McDonald's anyway...

MARK. You use McDonald's?

LATA. I don't buy anything. But yes, I use their soap, their toilet paper... and I do so with clear conscience. Do we not get to use McDonald's in the Labour Party?

HILARY. Do we really need to discuss our use or non-use of McDonald's?

MARK. Public toilets were built to encourage people to walk around public areas without fear of being taken by embarrassment. Surely we still want people on our streets?

HILARY. Let's put a pin in that one – return.

LATA. The museum according to this goes.

HILARY. Yes.

MARK. We've already cut all permanent staff.

HILARY. Last year. And some volunteers stepped into the breach.

LATA. Which means it still costs – £15,000. Power. Light. Maintenance.

MARK. No, no the museum is important – it's a celebration of our heritage it's...

HILARY. Has anyone ever gone? Have you ever gone, Mark?

MARK. I actually opened the exhibit on the canal...

HILARY. When have you gone not for work? When have you taken your kids?

MARK. Kid.

HILARY. We cut support, they can set up as a charity if they'd like... Maybe you can assist them with the forms. The same is true for the library I'm afraid. Everything that can be a charity, should be a charity. There are some councils trying to run their swimming pools like charities too.

MARK. I think...

HILARY. It's a beautiful pool, we're not doing that.

LATA. Besides, there'd be all sorts of third-sector-type stuff that wouldn't be...

MARK. Museums, libraries, all gone...

HILARY. Mark, if it was down to you we'd keep everything, I understand why – in an ideal world I'd feel the same – but... this isn't ideal – and I want some backing here.

Next proposal.

MARK. No, no, I know it's not an ideal world, I really do – but... this feels very rushed and this isn't how we previously did this...

HILARY. Nothing is being agreed, I simply want your two's opening reactions before we... take it to the Labour group. And then of course there's the ninety-day public consultation. Which is always...

LATA. Meaningless.

HILARY. And I'm rushing through simply because I want time to talk about the properly contentious issues...

MARK. And what are the 'properly' contentious issues?

HILARY. Off the top of my... well...

LATA. I don't have notes for...

HILARY. Elderly care. Disabled care. Sure Start Centres.

That's where the savings can be substantial.

MARK. Finally.

Undoubtedly contentious.

HILARY. Sure Start Centres are going to be an arse-ache, agreed?

MARK. Agreed.

LATA. Why?

HILARY. Mothers.

We make the cuts we can there – I asked for three possible models – twenty, thirty and forty per cent – I want to go for twenty per cent, the highest we can go without having to close doors, where the only impact will be on staffing numbers and opening hours. But twenty per cent won't get us anywhere close to our target. Which means disabled care and elderly care need to be… the questions are going to be larger for them.

MARK. So – let's talk elderly care…

HILARY. It's about identifying where the cuts can be most seamlessly felt.

MARK. Let's talk elderly care.

HILARY. Actually, let's talk disabled care.

Scene Five

Committee meeting.

JULIE. Well, Chair…

We've had four calls reporting on the 'Tina loves Steve' graffiti artist. Turns out his name is Steve. And Tina might not share his feelings.

The person who wrote 'anal' above the 'access only' signs on the Trowbridge estate is still at large.

And then there's the Stop Keith Campaign.

Someone keeps writing 'Keith' under every stop sign we have.

As yet, we have no idea who Keith is.

Scene Six

SARWAN *stands in front of a toilet mirror.*

SARWAN. I am honoured to accept this honorary Scout membership. The Scouts were an organisation that included me and my brothers from a young age. Which in this town, then was... Shit. Shit. Don't sound like a racist.

Don't sound like a...

He takes out a handkerchief and wipes his face.

I am honoured to accept this honourary Scout membership.

I am determined to use this opportunity to fuck as many Girl Guides as I possibly can.

Scene Seven

A low-brow press conference.

MARK. This has been a long road for this Council. And I won't lie to you, it's been difficult. We live in an age of – cuts. This means there's a certain inevitability to the decisions we make. But this council is one that isn't afraid to make the hard decisions, if they're the right decisions. We are a working-class town, that is our strength – and, in the current climate, our weakness. The recession hit us harder than most. And because our local tax yield is not as high as some – central government cuts will disproportionately fall upon us... Something the Conservative Party are struggling to admit even after three years of this. That is, of course, not to make an excuse of what's ahead...

HELEN. Can you tell us what you're intending to cut?

MARK. Well, the first thing is all of us have agreed to another reduction in our allowances. The councillors' base-rate allowance will go from just over £10,000 a year, to just over

£7,000 with the leadership all taking deeper cuts – myself and Hilary as leader have agreed to halve our remaining special responsibility allowance.

DAVID. I've heard rumours that elderly care will be...

MARK. Listen, let's not... We are still implementing a thorough...

GRAHAM. I'll read you a list. How about that? I'll read you a list and you tell me whether something is likely to go or not.

MARK *grins*.

MARK. Yeah. Great. You read down a list, I'll wink if you have got something right...

There's laughter. LAURA *walks out onto stage. She's carrying library books.*

Honestly, it's a tough job but we're going to do it to the best of our ability – we're still working through things, as soon as I have something to tell you...

He notices LAURA.

I will tell you...

Hello.

LAURA. Hello.

MARK. Are you... okay?

LAURA. Yes. You're Mark. I remember you.

MARK. Shit. Yes. And you're Susan.

LAURA. Laura.

MARK. Yes. Laura.

LAURA. Susan is close.

I used to see you at the day centre.

I've just come from the library.

Is that likely to go?

MARK (*laughs*). Don't you start.

Did you get any books?

She looks at her books. So does he.

LAURA. I've got to go now. We have spaghetti Bolognese for dinner tonight.

It's my second-favourite dinner.

She walks away.

MARK. Well. That.

That.

Where was I? Graham's list.

Essentially, all I can tell you is I will tell you something as soon as I have something to say.

Scene Eight

JAKE's *bedroom. In* MARK's *house. It's night.*

JAKE. Okay, so I don't get it…

MARK. What don't you get?

JAKE. When she says her thing is she actually – does she actually know she's saving the day?

MARK. What do you mean?

JAKE. Does she know she's saying – boom – I'm going to save the day here? By calling him out. By making him – I mean, they leave because she knows who they are, right?

Does she know that by – revealing them – revealing to them that she knows them that they'll leave?

MARK. I don't know. It's a good question.

JAKE. It's the biggest question and no one asks it – not even Atticus.

MARK. Why's it the biggest question?

JAKE. Because it's made out to be this big heroic act – but actually it isn't because she doesn't know she's doing it...

MARK. Well, isn't her being there actually the heroic act?

JAKE. Anyone can be there. It's outwitting them that makes her the hero – no one says – Batman, what a dude, he watched that train crash kill fifty people, he was so 'there' you know? So 'there'?

MARK. Surely the correct analogy would be that Batman saved the people but inadvertently – without meaning to – isn't the point the lives saved?

JAKE. No, the point is the intention. You've got to mean to do it, otherwise you're just lucky.

MARK. You should write all this down. For your essay.

JAKE. Mr Taylor doesn't want to hear about Batman.

MARK. He would if you're making a really coherent point.

JAKE. No. He wouldn't.

Pause.

MARK. I'm really pleased you engaged with the book so much, it was my favourite book when I grew up.

JAKE. Really? This book? But it's so pointless. Everything is so on the level. And it's all white people saving black people which is basically the liberal prejudice all of us buy in to.

MARK. I think in this case Tom Robinson did need saving.

JAKE. But maybe that mindset is what caused it all in the first place. I think everyone should be encouraged to save themselves.

MARK. I'm not sure...

JAKE. You saved yourself.

MARK. Not strictly... true.

Pause.

So... how have you been?

JAKE. Fine.

MARK. How's things at your mum's?

JAKE. Fine.

MARK. How's school? How's everything – there?

JAKE. Fine.

MARK. How are your friends?

JAKE. I've got friends. If that's what you mean.

MARK. Have you got a girlfriend?

JAKE. I like how you built up to that.

MARK. What?

JAKE. It was deceptive, how you built up to that. I liked how you built up to that. No. I don't have a girlfriend.

MARK. Any girls you've been – I don't know – casually seeing?

JAKE. Is this the sex talk? Are we going to have to talk about contraception in a bit?

MARK. Your mother said...

JAKE. You've been talking to Mum?

MARK. She emailed.

JAKE. She emailed she wanted you to talk to me about sex?

MARK. Yes.

JAKE. Great. That's weird. I love it. Did you buy props?

MARK. What?

JAKE. For our talk. Have you bought some condoms to show me how to use them? Is there a cucumber in your bag? Maybe you went the whole hog and bought lubricant? This is all a bit late, Dad.

MARK. You've been visiting some websites and she thinks...

JAKE. Oh, it's the websites she…

She's been spying on my internet usage.

Interesting.

MARK. Jake… some of the stuff…

JAKE. If we continue this conversation I'm going to leave.

MARK. Jake…

JAKE. Honestly, to be clear, if we continue this conversation…
I will not be lectured to by anyone – but particularly I will
not be lectured to by you. I can be educated. I accept
education. You are my dad. You need to educate me. But a
lecture? From you? No.

MARK. This is just me – expressing a concern – about your
life.

These are some pretty violent – sexually violent websites
you're visiting.

JAKE. It's pointless. This is a pointless conversation.

MARK. Of course I'm not concerned about that. It's a
completely different thing.

JAKE. I've also been playing a lot of the trombone recently. For
band. We've got a concert coming up. Are you concerned
about that?

MARK. That's a different thing…

JAKE. It's a different activity. I lead a varied life. And if you
dare talk to me more about this, I will walk out this door and
you won't know where I go, and you know – you fucking
know – I will be very good at hiding – from both of you.

How dare she – how dare she look at my computer.

And then not have the balls to talk to me about it.

Pause.

Are you getting any sex?

MARK. No.

JAKE. As in no I'm not answering your question, you rude little shit or no, I'm not getting any?

MARK. The latter.

JAKE. Maybe I'm queer.

MARK. Are you?

JAKE. No. Maybe you're queer.

MARK. I'm not.

JAKE. Are you sure? Mum said there were times when you seemed almost physically repulsed by her body. So...

MARK. She said that?

JAKE. She says a lot of things. Maybe you should email her.

But you were drinking then... She's really proud of you now. She won't talk to you. But she keeps telling me how proud of you she is.

Which is her way of not revealing that she hates you. The same as you hate her.

MARK. I don't hate her.

JAKE. But people don't like to talk about hate.

I don't mind hate. And those websites are about hate. I'm aware of that. And I don't mind that. I think it's a healthy outlet – for my hate. And I certainly wouldn't enact any of them in real life. If that's what scares you.

I just like masturbating to them. They're disgusting. And I like it. Because I'm disgusting. And you're equally as disgusting. So don't even – don't even start.

They sit in silence.

MARK. Okay.

I won't...

Say any more.

Pause.

JAKE. Good.

Pause.

MARK. Are you okay, Jake?

JAKE. I'm not a black man in the segregated south, Dad, I don't need saving.

Pause.

MARK. Shall we get a pizza?

JAKE. Sure, I could eat a pizza.

Scene Nine

GEORGE's *house. The middle of the night.*

JULIE. Dad?

JULIE *descends the stairs.*

Dad? It's pretty late. Early.

She descends further.

Are you down here? Dad?

GEORGE. Yes. I'm here.

JULIE. What are you doing down here…

GEORGE. Making eggs.

JULIE. Dad…

GEORGE. The thing about getting old is that every strange act you perform is regarded as a potential act of senility. I am eccentric. I have always been eccentric. I remain eccentric. I like eggs.

JULIE. You need to sleep.

GEORGE. True.

But at the moment I'm not sleeping.

And I also need eggs.

JULIE. I'll leave you to it.

GEORGE. Incorrect answer.

JULIE. What is the correct answer?

GEORGE. To apologise and to join me.

JULIE. It's three a.m.

GEORGE. The trouble with having ageing parents is that they'll die soon.

And they use the prospect of you losing them as a means by which to get you to join them in their eccentricity.

I'm – how old am I? Seventy-six. When do normal people die nowadays? I'm guessing I'm nearing it, or past it? Christ, I'm depressing myself.

JULIE. I don't want eggs.

GEORGE. Tea?

JULIE. That'll wake me up. I actually have work in the morning. And Council in the evening.

GEORGE. Orange juice?

JULIE. Orange juice also wakes you up. Natural sugar.

GEORGE. Fresh-mint tea?

JULIE. We don't have any fresh mint.

GEORGE. What herbs have we got? Basil tea? Oregano tea? Ginger tea? I've actually heard of ginger tea – that's what all you awful wankers drink nowadays, isn't it?

JULIE. You actually like fresh-mint tea.

GEORGE. I do. But I'm eccentric naturally. I don't have to try. Sage tea? Paprika tea? I wonder what that'll be like.

JULIE. You told me – when I moved back in with you, you told me that you would be purely a housemate. Not a… whatever you are.

GEORGE. I lied. Did I lie? I lied.

JULIE. I'll have a glass of water, Dad.

GEORGE. Perfectly sensible choice. How's Mick?

JULIE. Mark.

GEORGE. How's the man that you're sleeping with?

JULIE. I know that you know his name is Mark.

We're not – by the way – having sex any more.

GEORGE. How is he?

JULIE. Why do you care?

GEORGE. Because I'm fascinated by him.

JULIE. Why are you fascinated by him?

GEORGE. Because he's such a limp dick.

And yet he's Deputy Leader of the Council.

JULIE. He's a good man, Dad, and he's having a hard time.

GEORGE. Wonderful. Why?

JULIE. Well, that's a difficult question to answer.

Essentially, Mark doesn't like doing anything wrong.

GEORGE *laughs*.

GEORGE. But that's what leadership is. You think I didn't make mistakes when I was Leader? He needs to learn to break some eggs.

JULIE. That's not…

That's not…

GEORGE. Is this the conversation where I remind you – haven't you realised you're better than these people yet? Haven't you realised it's time to make your mark?

JULIE. You don't even know what that means…

GEORGE. Of course I don't. That's for you to – work out with yourself.

Could be a speech, an act, a heroic death.

But it is time.

I say, as your father, as your housemate.

I say as a man who thinks you're the greatest thing since toast.

These people... You're too good for these people.

Take it from someone who knows.

JULIE. Okay, shut up and make your eggs, would you?

Scene Ten

Council offices.

HILARY. Hear ye. Hear ye.

Gather round.

Gather round.

No... Just a joke.

She smiles.

Okay.

So here is the provisional budget which I must remind you is purely for circulation within the Labour Group whilst discussions are ongoing. I think it makes for very exciting –

GINA. You lied to me. You fucking lied to me.

You lied.

HILARY. Gina... I don't know what you've heard but... nothing has been decided...

GINA. You lied.

She pours liquid all over HILARY*'s head.*

HILARY. What? What is this?

GINA. You just pissed all over us. So we're pissing back.

ACT THREE

Scene One

Council surgery.

LAURA. I used to work in McDonald's.

> I did the chicken and fish stand.

> The Nuggets, the McChicken Sandwiches, the Fillet of Fish.

> No one ever ate the Fillet of Fish.

> We always had to cook one especially.

JULIE. I love a Big Mac.

LAURA. But then things changed. A new manager was worried about me.

> So he changed me to cleaning the floors.

> And then he slipped.

> So he changed me to cleaning the street outside.

> Picking up the bubble gum.

> From where it stuck – on the pavement.

JULIE. That doesn't sound good.

LAURA. I live with my parents. I like living with my parents. But I meet my friends at the day centre.

JULIE. I actually live with my dad too.

LAURA. Would you like to spend all day with him – every day.

JULIE. No.

LAURA. I don't want you to shut the day centre.

> It's fun. We go bowling. We make things. We have discos.

JULIE. Yes. I understand that.

LAURA. Please don't shut my day centre.

Scene Two

MARK *and* JULIE *lie naked in his bed.*

JULIE. Okay?

MARK. Okay.

> *They lie in silence for a moment.*

Actually I'm good. I'd raise it so far as to say I'm good.

JULIE. I'm good too.

> *He turns and looks at her.*

MARK. I've missed you.

JULIE. Okay.

MARK. Okay?

JULIE. Okay.

> *Pause.*

MARK. So you've decided you like me, right? You've decided you like me again?

JULIE. I've decided I like what we just did.

MARK. That'll do.

> *Pause. She strokes his back.*

> *And then she stops – she examines his back.*

JULIE. You've got a hole in your back...

MARK. Have I?

JULIE. Can't you feel it...? I'm touching it now...

MARK. How deep is the hole...?

JULIE. I don't know.

Quarter of a centimetre.

It's about the size of a five-pence piece.

You hadn't felt it? You had no idea it was there?

MARK. No, I had no idea I have a hole the size of a five-pence piece. In my back.

JULIE. Half a five-pence piece maybe. But round, like a five-pence piece.

A half-sized five-pence quarter of a centimetre, maybe an eighth of a centimetre, hole.

MARK *laughs.*

MARK. It's increasingly sounding more like a dent than a hole.

JULIE *pulls herself up to all fours. She looks down at him with true tenderness. She examines him carefully with true tenderness.*

So I was thinking – maybe we could get some food or something this weekend? Or go for a walk? Or go to the cinema? I've got Jake – but he's got orchestra and then –

Beat. He turns and looks at her.

Or – not.

Maybe not.

Clearly not.

Pause.

JULIE. I do care about you, Mark.

I just – I've always thought that I –

MARK. You're still not sure.

JULIE. So can we just – can we just – for now – treat this as a one-night lapse?

MARK. A one-night lapse?

JULIE. Lapse is probably the wrong word.

MARK. Probably.

Pause.

JULIE. I do care about you, Mark – I've just got to shift – some things in my head.

Pause.

Come on, don't – are you angry?

MARK. No.

JULIE. You struggle to even admit you're angry, don't you?

MARK. What does that mean?

JULIE *says nothing*.

Would you sleep with me more regularly if I were to lose my temper more?

I can lose my temper.

I am actually quite angry, so…

JULIE. Sorry.

MARK. No need.

JULIE. But I am sorry.

MARK. It was a one-night lapse. And I'm grateful for it.

I can be grateful for it.

Pause.

Any idea what prompted it?

Maybe I can create a similar situation again. Am I sounding pathetic yet?

It was the piss, wasn't it?

You took me to bed because Hilary had piss poured on her.

JULIE. My dad thinks I'm wasting my time. In the Council. Everyone thinks he's the one who got me in when in truth he did everything in his power to get me to stay out. Doesn't want me to be like him. It's a pretty constant refrain.

MARK. My dad was an electrician on the railways. He thinks councillors are mainly fraudsters.

JULIE. It wasn't the piss.

MARK *looks at* JULIE.

MARK. Hilary is going mad, trying to work out who leaked it.

She doesn't understand things just leak sometimes. Someone left something on a photocopier, or said something in the pub or...

JULIE. You didn't leak it?

MARK. Why would I have leaked it?

JULIE. Sorry, I just assumed. Why wouldn't you?

Gina's your ex-wife.

MARK. And?

JULIE. And the mother of your child.

MARK. So?

JULIE. She visited the centre that morning and that afternoon she discussed cutting it?

MARK. She visited because Gina wanted a cake competition judging...

JULIE. And that afternoon she discussed cutting its funding entirely.

MARK. You think she scheduled the cake competition deliberately?

JULIE. People ask her to do stuff all the time.

MARK. Maybe this isn't the best time for this chat...

JULIE. She went this time and then six hours later, cut the arse out of the building...

MARK. Yeah. Because it was the right thing to do.

JULIE. Really? That's a bold phrase… 'The right thing to do.'

MARK. We're trying to make hard decisions. We're having to make hard decisions. Am I sounding angry yet?

Pause.

JULIE. Yeah.

The trouble is we've been making hard decisions for three years now and it gets quite boring, doesn't it? After a while? That phrase?

Scene Three

GINA. You see, the thing about public consultation is that what it mostly means is a clipboard getting dusty in a dusty room. No one who cares knows they're being consulted and those that don't care provided the answers the Council needs.

Public consultation generally – almost unanimously – backs the Council. Because the Council never really consults the public.

LAURA *comes on in a dalmation costume. She looks at* GINA, *and laughs.*

LAURA. I've always looked really silly in this.

She hands GINA *a dalmation costume too, which she changes in to.*

GINA (*with a grin*). Yes. You look entirely ridiculous.

The campaign was actually surprisingly easy.

We sort of kicked into gear straight away.

Mostly it involved collecting signatures.

LAURA. We stood in the high street. Beside Boots. We had lollipops for the children.

And then we moved on to McDonald's. We collected a lot of signatures.

GINA. But we wanted to make our final play – a bit of a show.

We hired a boat and went down the canal with the clients all rowing.

She's now in her dalmation costume. She puts on a nose.

What do you think?

LAURA *laughs*.

LAURA. You look worse than me.

Scene Four

Council surgery.

JULIE. How can I help?

SARAH. I'm here to complain about shutting the day centre for the disabled. The handicapped. Is that the right word? I'm never sure which is the right word.

Scene Five

LAURA. We all got quite wet. The helpers had to help when we carried it around the…

When we carried it around the…

GINA. The locks.

LAURA. The locks. They had to help when we carried it around the locks.

They were dressed – we all were dressed as 101 Dalmations.

Scene Six

Council surgery.

LATA. Can I just say how delighted I am that you've come to see me today. How's progress on the credit issues? Were the Citizens Advice Bureau useful?

KEITH. You shouldn't be shutting the day care for the spastics.

LATA. Oh, I wasn't expecting… No. Okay.

Scene Seven

GINA. When we got to shore, we were met by –

There's a guy called Charlie. He's partially deaf and has pretty severe learning difficulties. He can't actually keep rhythm, but he loves throwing his baton around. So he conducted a jazz group of local mates of mine playing the *101 Dalmations* theme tune and other stuff.

HILARY. Fuck.

LAURA. Everyone wanted to ask us questions.

HILARY. Fuck.

GINA. I was expecting local press, I wasn't expecting national.

We then walked through the town, still dressed as 101 Dalmations and presented our petition to the town hall.

LAURA. That night, we had fireworks. And hot dogs.

GINA. And it was fantastic.

HILARY. Fuck.

Scene Eight

There's a silence in Cabinet for a moment. They all look exhausted.

HILARY. Okay.

She thinks. She rubs her hands.

Okay, so it seems to be open season...

LATA. The public consultation has proved less than meaningless.

MARK. Just to say – I've had representations from more or less everyone.

I used to be lucky to get three people into my surgeries. And that includes Roy –

LATA. Roy. Still on about the graveyard?

MARK. Last week, I had thirty-three. Thirty-three people all of whom are compelled by their desire to help the less fortunate.

It's actually quite admirable.

HILARY. And we have petitions.

MARK. How many petitions?

LATA. The city farm have come to us with a petition of 150, the swimming pool with a petition of –

She checks through.

285. Mainly about the cutting of aqua classes for the elderly. And the kids' splash-and-play.

MARK. We should have some sort of league-table system. Maybe. For petitions received.

LATA. 24 for the public toilets.

MARK. Told you.

HILARY. Vengeful McDonald's employees perhaps.

LATA. 78 for the parks. 124 for the museum. 93 for the library.

None for the street lighting in Longbridge.

MARK. And that's why petitions aren't to be trusted.

LATA. The Sure Start Centres have 786 signatures. They've acted as a collective.

Withensea Home for the Elderly has 36 signatures, Tunstall 49, Calbot 92.

HILARY. And Gina –

LATA *looks at* HILARY *guiltily.*

LATA. And then there is Gina.

Gina is the most impressive of all.

Gina has collected 4,933 signatures by hand.

MARK. You should have prosecuted her for assault.

HILARY. No. I shouldn't.

LATA. And online…

There's been a bit of a Facebook thing.

And Twitter. The number is growing quite rapidly.

She's collected 74,573 signatures on YouGov.

HILARY. Fuck.

Scene Nine

GINA*'s office.*

GINA. Been a while since you've been here.

MARK. Yes. You've decorated.

GINA. No. Just cleaned.

MARK. This was Hilary's idea. I said it wasn't a good one.

GINA. Your breath smells of mints. You haven't...

MARK. Gina. Don't. Please. I've just been eating mints.

GINA. All I'm saying is...

MARK. I know what you're saying. Don't.

GINA. Jake needs someone at the moment and if you...

MARK. Don't.

GINA. He told me about your chat. Said you were really embarrassing and then took him for pizza.

MARK. I'm not here to talk about our son.

She eyes him angrily for a moment.

GINA. Okay. Then let's keep this official. As if Hilary had just sent anyone to clear her shit up. Let's just treat this as you being – anyone.

Pause.

MARK. I'm not going to try and justify the decision...

GINA. Aren't you?

MARK. It's hard times for everyone. And she thinks we can work with you to identify a charity who might pick up the slack.

GINA. Really? Mencap is broke – donations are way down. And if you're talking about a local charity – maybe in Kensington. If you cut this, you cut this. So I guess you're back to justifying it.

MARK. Let's not start this with such angry...

GINA. So – this can go one of two ways – you can either justify it on the basis of it being a bit expendable, in which case, you believe that my client base should be left in their homes. Or you can justify it as there being alternative care available.

MARK. She thinks that the current provision is old-fashioned.

GINA. Does she? She's visited once – to judge a cake competition.

MARK. Come on, Gina...

GINA. I find it interesting you keep using 'she' – cowardice on your part or genuine disagreement?

MARK. You know how I feel.

GINA. And you know how I feel. Have my private opinions been used to justify the closure of my day centre?

MARK. Fine. I'll say it. I think it's old-fashioned. So do you.

GINA. And were you kind enough to pass these thoughts on to Hilary?

MARK. I told her what you think – what you've said – yes.

GINA. And does that seem to you an appropriate thing to have done? To have oversimplified my opinions and used them in a budget meeting?

MARK. It didn't hinge on your opinion. It hinged on mine – mine and Hilary's – and it wasn't an easy decision to come to. You know how hard these cuts have been on everyone. We're simply trying to make the best decisions for the town... and I understand you're hurt but...

GINA. The history of the day centre is actually quite an interesting thing.

Before us – disabled people had two choices – twenty-four hours a day with parents, or twenty-four hours a day in a home or hospital.

And you've been in some of those hospitals.

MARK. Yes, I have, but...

GINA. I met one woman – she was blind – she was sixty – Polly was her name – she had mild learning difficulties. But the blindness combined with the difficulties meant she'd been in a hospital for fifty-five years. I got her out last year. A shared home and a day centre. And she really – she didn't flower exactly – she'd been thoroughly institutionalised – but she began to do a bit better.

MARK. And it's great you got her out...

GINA. The history of the day centre is the history of the deinstitutionalisation of the mentally disabled. Now – people say that day centres are alienating, that true integration is preferable – that our clients should be out in the real world – but the truth is, the real world is full of cunts. You know, Polly's favourite possession? A picture of her with Jimmy Savile.

MARK. That's great.

Jimmy Savile – I hope you mention that in one of your media briefings.

GINA. Don't make out like I'm enjoying this... There's an argument to be made about integration. There's an argument to be made about improving everything. But it requires funds you aren't prepared to give. These places aren't perfect – I'll give you that – but they're the best we've got. You aren't making an argument because you don't actually have an alternative to the care I provide.

MARK. And to prove your righteous anger – on Polly's behalf you poured piss over someone? Don't take the moral high ground here.

GINA. I don't need to take the high ground. I have it. And I have 224,331 signatures which prove it. Even Stephen Fry is backing us.

MARK (sarcastic). Stephen Fry. Wow. I'm impressed. Well, that's... Well, in that case...

You know some would claim that this holier-than-thou act is merely a helpful disguise for a middle-aged woman scared of losing her job.

GINA. Keep it professional, Mark.

You had to make choices. You made the wrong choices.

MARK. We're trying to do the best for this town.

GINA. You're a grown man, Mark, you're past the point where 'trying' is an appropriate fucking response to anything.

Scene Ten

LAURA *walks up behind* GINA.

GINA. It becomes addictive. After a while, watching your
petition numbers rise.

You watch them grow – sometimes they grow at only four or
five an hour and you think you're done – and then there's a
surge – someone's tweeted something – doesn't always need
to be a celebrity – a snooker commentator or a – and then a
hundred sign, and then a hundred grows quickly to two
hundred, and then that multiplies to a thousand.

LAURA. To a hundred thousand.

GINA. To a million.

LAURA (*laugh*). No. Not to a million. Not yet.

GINA. You get dry and wet patches essentially.

Some days I'd just sit and watch – watch the numbers grow
– and it's hugely satisfying.

I was viral. I was a virus. Pictures retweeted of Laura in a
dalmation costume became a virus – became an epidemic.

The *Independent* came to take our picture.

They requested the costumes of course.

Scene Eleven

HILARY *sits alone in her office.*

She thinks. She thinks again.

MARK *enters.*

MARK. Hi.

HILARY. Hello.

MARK. My phone literally doesn't stop ringing.

HILARY. Mine is on silent.

So most calls go straight to voicemail.

I got my nephew to re-record my message last night.

He says 'Roses are read, bogeys are green, please leave a message on this stupid machine.'

Seems to have cut out most of the abuse.

Some of the abuse.

MARK *sits*.

I've been told – in no uncertain terms – that if her petition hits a million Ed will make a statement condemning this Council and possibly cutting us off.

Her petition currently stands at 714,887.

MARK. Hilary…

HILARY. I asked whether the leadership understood anything of what we were going through. I asked her whether Ed could advise.

She said we had her sympathy but that I had to understand every second question he's getting is about us and it's distracting people from the run-up to the election campaign.

MARK. What?

HILARY. We're diluting the message. We're polluting it. We're making it about disabled people and they haven't agreed a disabled-people message.

They're embarrassed by us.

MARK. Well…

HILARY. I get phone calls which tell me I'm embarrassing.

We've got to do something. We've got to stop Gina.

This is about survival now.

MARK. Hilary… we can't give her what she wants…

HILARY. We have no choice.

She's won.

We're keeping her open.

I need to find some other cuts.

We do.

You need to be with me on this, Mark. I need you with me.

Scene Twelve

SARWAN's *bench.*

HILARY. I've always admired your choice of bench, it's remarkably – central.

SARWAN. I'd like to think I chose it – but – in truth – it chose me – very alluring it was. Come do your paperwork here, it said – whispered.

HILARY. I hear you gave a very entertaining speech to the Scouts the other day.

SARWAN. How did you hear that?

HILARY. My nephew. He's in the 4th Regiment. I do hate that they call them regiments. Anyway, he was quite – he is quite a fan of yours. Said he didn't realise people from the Council could be funny. Which I tried not to be insulted by.

SARWAN. They gave me a woggle. What do you want, Hilary?

HILARY. A catch-up. A general catch-up.

SARWAN. That's very unlike you.

HILARY. Maybe I'm trying to change.

So... how have you been?

SARWAN. Really? Terrible. I've got this itching. I think it's a
rash. I think I'm maybe only a day away from seepage. Can I
show it you?

HILARY. Fine. I'll get to the matter in hand.

The day-centre problem.

We're being pressured nationally by the party.

SARWAN. I hope you're feeling the local pressure too. It's
wrong. It shouldn't be shut.

HILARY. Quite. So we're trying to think of alternatives that
will provide us with the replacement savings...

SARWAN. Why don't you just say the Conservatives are
wankers?

HILARY. Sarwan –

SARWAN. I would make clear they've caught us in a trap. We
can't raise council tax. We can't cut ring-fenced services.
The richer – largely Tory – councils – raise the majority of
their revenue from other sources. They have parking and
business rates. These cuts have fallen disproportionately on
working-class towns. It's class war, Hilary, it's that simple. I
would tell people that – I would tell people what they're
doing.

HILARY. People voted for us to lead – not to moan.

SARWAN. No one knows what's going on. I tell my friends –
and once they understand...

HILARY. Mark and I have agreed: Gina stays open.

We're going to be cutting some Sure Start Centres.

SARWAN. Right. Okay.

HILARY. Once we get the consent of the Labour Group...

We're going to shut – we're going to shut four Sure Start
Centres. We're shutting two in Binkley Down.

Beat. SARWAN *looks at her. Assessing her.*

SARWAN. Okay. You're shutting two in the largely Pakistani and Bangladeshi area, interesting.

HILARY. This is based on thorough statistical analysis.

This is based on an Equalities Impact Assessment.

This is based on – numbers of attendees and growth statistics – there will still be one operating in the area.

And one operating in West Park too. Which we will lay on buses to.

SARWAN. You're suggesting that – do you know about West Park? Do you know about the EDL's presence there?

HILARY. I have no choice. I have to listen to the numbers. Otherwise it is reverse racism, isn't it?

Anyway, I need your help...

SARWAN. Hilary, you can't be...

You can't do this.

HILARY. The only way it's possible to justify cutting any is by sticking to rigid statistical analysis. Which leads to two being cut in Binkley.

SARWAN. And the Labour core vote won't be largely affected.

And most of our voters are slightly racist and so won't mind.

In fact, it might lead us to stealing a few votes back from Ukip.

HILARY. You can take this to the mosque, you can help...

SARWAN. I can be of no help to you on this.

HILARY. Sarwan, you're a member of our Council, you're a Party member.

I can help you get on the Budget Steering Group next time. With a few adjustments. I can bring you onto some key teams.

SARWAN. Hilary, you're a cunt.

HILARY. No. I...

SARWAN *stands up and walks away.*

Sarwan, I should be the one walking away...

After you called me that I should be the one walking away...

But I'm still...

Here.

Please. Come back. It's based on statistics. We've got to do...

Sarwan, are you listening to me?

Sarwan, we're doing this.

Scene Thirteen

GINA*'s kitchen. She opens a bottle of champagne.*

It pours over most of the stage.

JAKE. You're going to need to wash that floor.

GINA *laughs, delighted.*

Scene Fourteen

A larger press conference.

MARK. These have been hard decisions, particularly on the
Sure Start rationalisations, but buses will be available to
make Sure Start available to all. There will also be some cuts
to elderly care, but with moving care into the home, maybe
we can give greater independence. We believe this town –

HELEN. So the Sure Start cuts will stand? You're not going to back down again?

MARK. This is a made budget – yes. The Labour Group have voted on it and we will officially pass it in the next full Council session.

HELEN. We were led to believe the budget with the disability day centre was also –

MARK. The cuts to the day centre were only provisional and were reappraised. These cuts have been carefully considered. And yes – are no longer provisional. If you'll let me continue – we believe this town…

DAVID. Do you have a message for Eric Pickles?

MARK. What's he said now?

DAVID. He's said this Council doesn't know its arse from its elbow.

MARK. This coming from a man whose arse is six feet wide?

They all write that down.

No. No. That was a joke. Come on. That was a joke. None of you are laughing but it was a joke. Don't write it down. Please don't print it.

Listen, let's not… blow this out of perspective. This is a working-class town that needs to work together to –

GRAHAM. To do what?

MARK. To survive.

GRAHAM. Doesn't seem like we're surviving to me, Councillor – does it to you?

Scene Fifteen

MARK*'s house.*

JULIE. Mark… Are you there?

> *Beat.*

> Mark…

> You better not be hiding from me…

> *Beat.*

> Mark…

> You may think you're –

> What do you think you are?

> What are you even doing this for?

Scene Sixteen

Council surgery.

LATA. It was a tough one.

SAUL. It's a disgrace is what it is. My kid used to love going to his Sure Start Centre.

> And then he comes home – a ball of tears – telling me his Sure Start is now – no offence, love – full of fucking Asians.

Scene Seventeen

Council surgery.

JULIE. Listen, I'm not going to say that this is not something we didn't agonise over, you...

CHRIS. Explain to me who I vote for now? I can't vote Lib Dem. I can't vote you. Who do I vote for now? Nigel Farage?

Scene Eighteen

SARWAN*'s bench.*

SARWAN. Snickers?

MARK. No. I'm okay.

SARWAN. Fine, I'll eat two.

Will you sit with me while I eat them?

MARK. I sort of need to...

SARWAN. I need you to sit with me.

MARK *sits.* SARWAN *eats a Snickers.*

Just so you know...

There's already talk of a march.

MARK. When?

SARWAN. Saturday.

And the English Defence League are talking of doing a counter-march in support of our measures. We're being defended by the EDL.

Because they believe – like we do – that brown children don't deserve Sure Start Centres.

MARK. I don't think...

SARWAN. And if you think there won't be violence...

MARK. I don't think we should be bullied by marches on either side.

SARWAN. You almost sound like you believe it.

It's time to act, Mark.

MARK. And do what?

SARWAN. A mass resignation. Cut her ground from under her...

MARK. I think you'd be misinterpreting events quite seriously if you thought this was all about one woman's decisions.

SARWAN. She calls you her glue, did you know that?

MARK. Yes.

SARWAN. Because you're a little bit left and a little bit right and people think you've got a conscience as a result. Because you're a recovering alcoholic so a bit weak, but also as Deputy Leader – strong. Because you're so nice and yet can be a wanker when you want to be.

MARK. Great. Thanks for summing me up.

SARWAN. I've known people dependent on glue. I grew up in places you can't even dream about.

MARK. As always you're marvellously eloquent, Sarwan. But I'm pretty sure you grew up in a more affluent community than I did.

SARWAN. And yet neither of us grew up in areas this Government would give a shit about.

You know, there was an article in the paper – Hart Council in Hampshire, the least deprived local authority – net loss of these cuts £28 per person – while in Liverpool District B, the most deprived local authority – net loss £807 per person. How does that not make you want to tear someone's throat out?

MARK. At the moment, I try to avoid reading papers.

SARWAN. We can be the first council under this Government that refuses to make a budget.

That refuses to accept their cuts.

MARK. What?

SARWAN. Let's refuse it. Let's refuse it all.

MARK. And have them replace us?

SARWAN. Our comrades in the eighties refused to set one. They were threatened with surcharges. They stood strong. We should do the same.

MARK. The law has changed since then. Local Government Finance Act 1988, I've looked into it, Sarwan.

SARWAN. Section 114. So have I. Our Chief Finance Officer will have to report us for financial mismanagement. And then a budget will probably be made without us. I'm aware of all this.

MARK. Then...

SARWAN. Let them try – we can take the people with us on this. We can – we can do a Gina. Just say no. Just say we've had enough. Be strong. Not weak.

MARK. We're a small council.

SARWAN. All it takes for great change to happen is for a butterfly to flap its wings.

I know all about that from India. And as a man who came close to becoming an ethnic minority himself recently, you must understand too...

MARK. Scotland? They lost, Sarwan. And had I been able to vote, I'd have voted for – for the benefit of the Party.

SARWAN. A mistake. Eighty-five per cent turnout. Young engagement. They wanted to change their country. That's beautiful. 'I am the forty-five per cent.'

MARK *smiles*.

Hilary is not going to budge. You know this, I know this.
She likes power too much. And the Labour Group will
always vote her policies through. It's the trouble with being
so overwhelmingly Labour. So a mass resignation – that's
the way.

A splinter group – behind you – I'd be able to persuade
seven, ten councillors to come with us, and once they
come... Once they come.

The whole pack of cards will come crumbling down.

What Cameron and his cronies have done is gut us.

With the spotlight on this town now – we can really show the
country what they've done. What it means.

As Nye Bevan said, 'We know what happens to people who
stay in the middle of the road. They get run down.'

We've been run down. Now we need to... you know...

We're the Labour Party.

Together. United. We'll never be defeated.

Scene Nineteen

MARK *lines up four glasses. He pinches his nose and does a
nasal newsreader's voice.*

MARK. Violence broke out today after members of the Muslim
community and EDL supporters clashed over...

He pours whisky into all four. He pinches his nose again.

Violence broke out today after a school bus filled with Asian
schoolchildren was stopped by white fascists who...

He looks at them all.

Violence broke out at the school gates today as parents
picking up their children...

And then one by one he tips them over.

*Until the last one which he thinks about a beat – maybe two
beats – and then drinks.*

Scene Twenty

HILARY's *office.* HILARY *is on the phone.*

HILARY. No. We didn't panic. We made a rational decision,
that some people like and some people don't.

Yes. Yes. I understand you're angry...

I understand and yet – and yet –

Please don't shout at me.

Okay. I'm putting the phone down now. I'm putting the
phone down.

*She puts the phone down. She sits, overwhelmed for a
moment.*

And then there's a knock at the door.

Come in.

LATA *enters. There's a silence.*

LATA. It was me. Told her. Leaked it to Gina. It was me.

HILARY. Ah.

LATA. I thought – I thought it was good politics – I thought I
was helping – I thought I could get her on-side without any
of the issues – I mean, with Mark being – and not wanting to
leave you exposed. And we used to be friendly – back in the
day. I thought I could get her on-side before the
announcement. So it wouldn't all – blow up. And then she
poured piss on you.

HILARY. I'll be very interested to know why you thought you could persuade her...

LATA. I thought if she could understand – I thought I could get a head start on her understanding before any of the press could... before the public consultation...

It was stupid.

So... I think I should resign. So you can bring Sarwan on to the steering group. For these latest cuts. The Sure Start cuts. That haven't been going so... I think he might be able to take it to the mosques in a way that – I can't. I think – I'm not one for racial profiling as you know – but I think you need a Muslim beside you on this one.

For the good of the Party, you know?

For the good of the town.

Pause.

HILARY. How did you get into politics, Lata? What drew you in?

LATA. I was a shop steward. Unison.

HILARY. Yes. Yes. I knew that. I suppose my question is more – why? A tendency towards public service? A need to impress people? Maybe you enjoy being able to call yourself a councillor. Or maybe you simply have a fetish for committee meetings?

LATA *thinks*.

LATA. My mother wasn't a strong woman. My father was – occasionally quite brutal with her. She let him. She let the world happen to her. I think we need to make the world we live in.

HILARY *looks up – slightly moved – she smiles*.

HILARY. A good answer.

LATA. And you – why did you?

HILARY. Nothing so profound I'm afraid.

I was a school governor. Never had any kids. People thought I'd be good at it. And one thing led to another...

It's a strange thing really, isn't it? To care this much? Feels profoundly old-fashioned.

I like that – about making the world.

Thanks for the offer, Lata. But it really won't be necessary.

Scene Twenty-One

Outside MARK*'s house.*

JAKE. You're Julie. From the Council.

JULIE. You're Jake, Mark's son.

JAKE. You here to wait for him?

JULIE. Yes.

JAKE. I think he forgot it was my day – that he was supposed to pick me up from school.

JULIE. How did you get here?

JAKE. I walked.

JULIE. From Waltham High? That's a way.

JAKE. You know which school I go to?

JULIE. I work with your dad, I know things...

JAKE. It's about seven miles, yes. And we've been told to take care. Because of the violence at the moment.

Because the town is all antsy.

Do you think he's having a really quiet breakdown?

JULIE. No. What are you reading?

JAKE. *Catcher in the Rye*.

JULIE. Good book, where you at?

JAKE. It's like the eighth time I've read it, I'm not really reading it for the story any more.

JULIE. What are you reading it for?

JAKE. I'm studying it. For words. For the words he uses.

JULIE. Okay. You want to be a writer?

JAKE. No. I just want to work out how he uses words.

JULIE. Okay.

JAKE. I heard him crying – last time I stayed.

Either crying or wanking.

I heard these gasps of air. You know those gasps of air people make?

Like they're having a panic attack. Or a wank.

JULIE. I'm pretty sure he's not having a breakdown. I'd know if he was having a breakdown.

JAKE. Are you two shagging again?

JULIE. No.

JAKE. Because he said he wasn't shagging

JULIE. We're not shagging.

JAKE. Your top's too tight – and you're wearing a lacy bra – don't girls only wear lacy bras when they're shagging? Are you sure you're not shagging him?

She says nothing. He reads off her look.

Good because you're twenty years younger than him and prettier than him and frankly, it'd probably be more appropriate for you to be shagging me than him.

JULIE. Sixteen years and I prefer older men.

JAKE. And it's such a cliché. Younger woman falls for older wiser man. At least he's not powerful, if he was powerful that'd truly take the biscuit, we know for a fact he's not powerful. Do you know how much I get the piss taken out of me for my dad working for the Council? I'm known as 'The Councillor', at school.

And the wise-man thing is also a joke.

Older men are not wiser men, they're just more attuned to their own failure and that makes them seem wiser.

JULIE. You're very clever, aren't you?

JAKE. I'm devastatingly clever.

JULIE. What do you want to be? When you grow up?

If not a writer...

JAKE. Something in marriage guidance.

JULIE. That's a very clever thought – you're very clever.

And yet – despite all your – cleverness – you can't stop staring at my tits which makes you a classic teenage, over-masturbating, spotty little shit, doesn't it?

JAKE. I've hurt you. I apologise. Was it the marriage-guidance stuff?

JULIE. What?

JAKE. I didn't think the marriage-guidance answer was particularly clever.

JULIE. You and your dad have more in common than you think, you know?

JAKE. How many times has he asked you 'Am I a good man?'

JULIE *turns and looks at him.*

Mum says he still calls her – when he's drunk – when he falls off the wagon – which he does by the way – if you didn't know – and asks her that. Am I a good man? It's pathetic. He's pathetic.

JULIE. He's your dad.

JAKE. And I love him but it doesn't make him any less pathetic. He wants to save people not because he should save people but because he wants to feel good. It's pathetic. I'm getting it written on his gravestone. That and 'alcoholism is the most boring of all the "isms", other than maybe socialism.'

Personally – I think cowardliness is too often mistaken for niceness and goodness.

Sometimes people don't act – don't confront – because they're scared too. Not out of any innate...

I think Dad gets confused by that.

Like I say, I love him.

Pause.

I'm sorry if I was rude to you.

JULIE. I was pretty rude to you.

JAKE. I'm outrageously bullied at school – I mean, really fucking brutally – as you probably know because Dad has probably told you – rudeness doesn't bother me – it sort of rolls off.

Pause.

But that's no excuse for being rude to you.

Pause.

What are you here for? If it's not for a shag?

JULIE. I'm here to try to...

To talk him into doing something brilliant. To standing up and being counted. What are you here for?

JAKE. I'm here because I have to be. It's his day. I'm quite a stickler for rules.

Beat.

You want to sit down? I've been sitting on his free newspaper because I'm petrified of piles, but you can have it if you want – the free newspaper.

JULIE. I can just sit. My arse is bigger than yours.

JAKE. That is undoubtedly true.

Scene Twenty-Two

Labour Party offices.

GEORGE. Thanks for seeing me.

MARK. Thanks for coming in.

It's an honour to have you here. What you did for this town...

GEORGE. No need for the guff. It's appreciated, but no need for the guff. I don't know if you mean it and I don't really care if you do. I'm grateful for your time. I know you're busy. I appreciate your time.

MARK. My pleasure.

GEORGE. Listen, my daughter is in a state about all this...

MARK. If you're here to –

I'm trying to treat your daughter well and I don't think she'd like her father coming here and telling me –

GEORGE *stops. He frowns.*

GEORGE. Are you telling me you've been treating my daughter badly?

MARK. No.

GEORGE. Good. Because I'm not here to talk about that...

Unless. What have you done to her?

MARK. Nothing.

I – what are you here to talk about?

GEORGE. I was a councillor for thirty-two years. I was Leader through the late seventies.

That was – that was a bleak time. It was red versus red. The winter of discontent was... pretty brutal. I thought I might be able to give you some – insight – during this time.

MARK. 'Insight'?

GEORGE *looks at* MARK.

GEORGE. Sarwan is a friend of mine. He came to see me. With Julie. And I'm not sure things are quite as clear as he... as she...

I'm not sure things are that straightforward.

Or not as straightforward as they'd like them to be.

But I know the decision as to what happens next doesn't really rest with Sarwan, or my daughter, it rests with you.

You're on the wire with this one.

MARK. I am.

GEORGE. So I thought you might like to talk to an old-time wire-walker...

MARK. You're here to give me advice?

GEORGE. Yes.

MARK. Okay.

GEORGE. You're making me feel like I'm being grossly inappropriate...

MARK. No. I'm just – slightly confused...

GEORGE. What's confused you?

MARK. Well, to be frank, I'm confused because I don't know you very well and because you've always made relatively clear – whenever I have met you – that you don't like me very much. In fact, I'm pretty sure this is the longest conversation we've ever had. But please – go ahead – with the advice. I am interested.

GEORGE. Okay. My advice is 'sod them'.

MARK. What?

GEORGE. Sod them.

MARK. You may need to unpack that statement slightly for me, George.

GEORGE. I admire George Osborne. And not just for his astute name rebranding. I even admire David Cameron.

MARK. George, are you drunk?

GEORGE. Because in their own way – by their own terms – they've succeeded extremely well. They have rebranded Britain, they have remade the British economy. Not in a way I'd like – but by their own standards – they've knocked it out of the park. Last year the IMF said we were heading for disaster – this year – they predict a growth surge of three-point-two per cent by the end of the year.

MARK. I think this town is proof that this growth doesn't exist nationwide...

GEORGE. But they don't care about our town. Never have. They're very consistent on that.

The figures are distorted by the Euro crisis and money movement and all sorts else – but for their friends – they've done very very well indeed. We – the Labour Party – we've been less successful.

MARK. That's a bold statement.

GEORGE. The truth is our Party doesn't fit the modern world.

MARK. That's a bolder one.

GEORGE. The way I think about it was the twentieth century was a great big experiment with social democracy. The twenty-first has revealed that such a thing is impossible.

MARK. You think the banks' collapse was about the collapse of socialism? Because I don't want to pop your balloon, George, but...

GEORGE. No, I think what followed the collapse did.

MARK. You're talking about the recession? The recession wasn't – socialist enough for you – ?

GEORGE. No, I'm talking about the absence of protest. Where were the marches? Where were the marches protesting a coalition government making sweeping changes that its lack of electoral mandate should have made impossible? There were a few, yes. But compared to what we used to be capable of? It was pitiful. The students marched, rioted in fact, a few other people marched. But mostly – people stayed at home and looked after themselves. And where they did protest – the protests were so – the protests were so simple. The odd library was kept open. The odd – day centre. We should be burning their buildings from underneath them. For what they've done. For how they behaved.

MARK. That sounds quite an old-fashioned means of protest, George – maybe in today's world we're slightly more – sophisticated – than that.

GEORGE. Iceland revolted. Greece went wild. But Ireland – the UK – places where the Government took on severe debt from the bankers. I mean, Ireland went to the fucking wall... People stayed at home. Why? Because they're sophisticated?

MARK. No. Because –

GEORGE. Because we – the Labour Party, the Labour movement – don't really – ultimately – have the believers any more. Or maybe our believers just don't know how to believe any more.

MARK. I'm not sure that's true. And I'm pretty sure cynicism towards party politics affects the Tories as badly as us. It's why Farage – is proving such a successful –

GEORGE. But the Tories never needed believers. Solidarity means fuck-all to them. Mutual self-interest is all that matters to them. For us – it's all we have. It's all we've ever had. Because without it... what are we? What can we mean?

MARK. I understand solidarity matters. I really do. And I think you make some good points about why it's gone but...

GEORGE. The Tories want to make dependence-culture a thing of the past, they want to convince us we can't afford to help those in need. But their greatest achievement is they've convinced us to turn on each other. So instead of shouting as one at them, we're shouting at each other. Instead of screaming in protest at the bankers for stealing millions from them, we're reporting our neighbours for ten pounds of benefit fraud.

Idealism is dead. Solidarity is dead. It's been destroyed by pragmatism and hatred and shame.

My point is – all of us in this Party – we're wasting our time. We've wasted our time. Our lives some of us.

And I've tried to work – I've been thinking about when we lost our belief – how we lost our believers – because we did – they didn't desert us, we lost them.

Maybe it was Iraq, maybe it was Clause 4, maybe Blair, maybe Kinnock...

MARK. Maybe it all goes back to the Jarrow March?

GEORGE. But the good thing is – for you is – we – you – we don't represent anything any more – so be free of it. You only have one responsibility – not to the Party, not to the country, not to Ed Miliband, not even to the working class – your sole responsibility is to this town. You only have to be good – to this town. Make the good decision – for this town.

Beat.

MARK. And what is the good decision?

GEORGE. Well, son, that's a battle I can't fight for you...

You need to work out good for yourself. Tough as it is.

Not that it ever was that clear – but that particular pond – the good pond – right now, it's murky as hell. For you. For everyone.

MARK *tries to digest this.*

MARK. I don't know what you're asking me to do.

Beat.

GEORGE. I'm asking you to be a great man.

And I've not the slightest idea what that involves.

And I've not the slightest idea whether you're capable of it.

Scene Twenty-Three

Council chambers. Corridor. MARK *sits.*

SARWAN *runs in.*

SARWAN. A Pakistani shopkeeper has been found dead.

    JULIE *runs in, in floods of tears.*

JULIE. Mark... Mark...

    LATA *enters and stands at the sidelines.*

SARWAN. Stabbed seven times with a kitchen knife.

MARK. Shit.

JULIE. Our first fatality.

LATA. 'Our' might be taking it too far...

JULIE. You don't think we did this?

    LATA *takes a step back.*

LATA. We don't know that we did this. Did we do this?

MARK. White? Were they white – were they EDL?

JULIE. They don't know.

MARK. Was it because of the marches?

SARWAN. We don't know – no one saw the assailant – it was pretty dark.

    But – he was killed in Longbridge, Mark.

    Pause. MARK *looks up wretchedly.*

MARK. Where we'd turned off the lights.

SARWAN. Where we'd turned off the lights.

Twenty-Four

SARWAN. Point of order, Chair. Before the debate continues, I wish to announce, on a matter of principle, my resignation from the Council.

HILARY. Councillor, perhaps...

JULIE. Point of order, Chair, I also wish to announce, on a matter of principle, my resignation from the Council.

Beat.

HILARY. Well, before this continues perhaps we could...

MARK. Point of order, Chair, I also wish to announce, on a matter of principle that I too hereby resign my membership of the Council.

HILARY. Mark?

LATA. Point of order, Chair.

I also wish to announce that...

I am also here to...

I am to here...

Well, I think we need to – I think this might be...

I hereby resign my membership of the Council.

Beat.

HILARY. Fine.

ACT FOUR

Scene One

SARWAN. If I had to tell you what a council exists to do I'd
start by saying that I believe good councils are – and bear
with me on this because it will be entirely worth it – bridges.
On the top you have the sleek cars – moving fast from one
direction to another – needing swift and good governance.
And medium cars – moving medium-fast. And bikes –
moving at bike speed. On the bottom you have homeless
people, junkies, graffiti artists and young rutting teenagers.
Our job is to help those on the top and those at the bottom,
all whilst watching the young rutting teenagers. And that, my
friends, is what a council does.

That actually was quite a decent metaphor in my head.

Not one of my best.

MARK. There was a kid at school. James Talbot. We went to
school and Scouts together. We liked each other in Scouts,
but in school – you can't be friends with who you want to be
friends with in school. James was a victim of some bullying,
and I didn't want to be contaminated.

JULIE. To provide access to democracy. People struggle to
meet their MP, meeting their councillor is and should be
easy. They should feel direct access. They should feel the
decisions around them – whether it be the positioning of
traffic lights or money for the provision of care for the
elderly – are something they can have a direct impact on.

MARK. So instead of being friends with James – I became
friends with his bullies. In particular this guy called Toby
Jenkins. Who hated James. Really hated him. Never really
understood why.

There was this shop in town called Round Pounds. I
happened to know James bought some of his clothes from

there – James told me in Scouts – he told me his dad was impressed with how well-made some of the clothes were – and that's what I told Toby.

HILARY. Councils exist to run things that need to run locally.

It's that simple.

MARK. So Toby started this song, 'Round Pounds' to the tune of 'Downtown' by – is it Lulu? 'Round Pounds, James buys all his clothes from there, Round Pounds, he even asked if they'd cut his hair, Round Pounds.' You know the sort of thing.

JULIE. She rejected our resignations. Of course.

She worked with us to draft a statement which stated that we will not be making a budget, because it's impossible to make a budget.

MARK. One day we were all pulled in for a big assembly. A big assembly on bullying. The headmaster, a nervous man, said that he wasn't going to identify any of the culprits, but he knew who they were – a strange position to take, I thought even then. He said he wasn't going to put up with it. He said we were to look to our consciences. And as he said that I looked across at Toby – who was laughing, I smiled back. It wasn't until later that we saw what had prompted it – James came back into school – and he had a big chunk of his hair missing. He'd pulled it out, in the night, we found out. He was that traumatised by our stupid song.

SARWAN. We'll spin the dice. We'll wait for Twitter to back us.

We'll wait for anyone to back us.

MARK. Responsibility. You can either take responsibility or you can't. You can either acknowledge your own power, or you can stick your head in the ground and decide you've got no responsibility.

LATA. Eric Pickles – Minister for Communities – believes that councils exist…

Well, I'm not sure what Eric Pickles think councils exist to do.

His fifty ways to save – a list he did for local councils –
included helpful tips such as 'cut back on first-class travel'.
Did we ever do that? And 'open a pop-up shop in spare
office space'. Or 'cancel glitzy award dos'. Or 'stop
translating documents into foreign languages'. Well, yes, but
then most of the women in Pakistani and Bangladeshi homes
in our town – who speak English but who don't read it very
well – will be cut off – will be – will be forced to be more at
the behest of their husbands. And, for me, councils are about
– access to power. Power you can feel. Power you can see.
Power you can feel – part of.

My mother didn't read English

SARWAN. I'm not very good at waiting.

I don't like surprises or suspense.

Give me a nice body horror over a suspense film.

Give me... *The Human Centipede* over *North by Northwest*,
you know?

Actually *The Human Centipede 2* is a bit of a classic.

MARK. We've called this press conference to tell you that our
Council has refused to agree a budget. Not failed. Not any of
those words. Refused. And I'll tell you why – because what
this Government is doing – and this is beyond politics – to
local authorities amounts to nothing more than barbarism.
They are cutting our money and not allowing us to replace it
with local tax rises. And this money – is money we need for
essential services. Not just services – essential services.
Particularly in the poorer areas of this country – the poorer
areas like this one. This country gets richer every day but as
our nation's wealth grows, so does our nation's wealth
inequality. And behaviour like this – the behaviour they've
shown towards this Council – only serves to exacerbate that
problem. As the party in power they have a responsibility to
the people of this country. A responsibility that they are
failing to meet. They are failing to meet it because they
choose to fail. It is a choice. And we are choosing not to –
we are choosing not to –

He takes a breath. He looks up.

We are choosing not to subsume ourselves to their irresponsibility. We're choosing to take responsibility for the mistakes we've made. We're choosing to take responsibility for the future of this town. And we're throwing this problem back to them – we say – we say – we need more. And you need to acknowledge that.

JULIE *enters carrying newspapers. She starts to go through them.* MARK *takes a few more.*

JULIE. The newspapers are in… We're in all of them.

LATA. And Twitter has started to… Twitter has started to…

We're trending.

SARWAN. Sky News. We're on Sky News.

HILARY. Go on then.

What does everyone say?

Scene Two

SARWAN *answers his door in his dressing gown to* GINA.

SARWAN. Gina.

GINA. Sarwan.

SARWAN. What are you doing here?

GINA. I'm here as your constituent actually.

SARWAN. Okay. Okay. I can cope with that. I'm sort of –
    dissolved at the moment. And this is sort of my front door.
    But I can cope with that. How can I help you?

GINA. I had to talk to you because I don't like anyone else.

SARWAN. Then I take it as a massive compliment that you've
    interrupted my sleep.

GINA. I don't understand what's happened.

SARWAN. We resigned, Hilary capitulated, we came back together to refuse to make a budget. We are obliged by law to make one. In the absence of it our budget-making abilities are being acquired by another – appointed by Westminster.

GINA. So – what's going to happen next?

SARWAN. Big things.

We hope.

GINA. And the day centre?

SARWAN. We're hoping they're going to be embarrassed enough to raise our central allowance. We're hoping the press and Twitter will... We're hoping things will turn around and people will... support us.

No one's ever done this before, Lewisham came close, Stoke flirted with it.

This is uncharted territory. We're off the grid.

We just need popular support.

GINA. But people hate you. The press hate you.

Beat. SARWAN *looks up at her. For the first time unsure.*

SARWAN. Yes. Yes. There is that.

Yes.

I thought they'd like us more than they – do.

Scene Three

MARK*'s bedroom.*

MARK *is getting dressed.*

JULIE *watches him.*

He turns and looks at her.

MARK. I like leaving you in my bed.

JULIE. Today is going to be fine.

MARK. No. It's not. But I like leaving you in my bed.

He makes to exit. And then he stops.

JULIE. I am proud of you.

MARK. You know, I always used to credit politics with saving me.

I used to go to the pub when I was... every night when I didn't want to...

And then I started going to meetings.

Gina hated it.

I got involved in a campaign at the university. And then someone on that committee asked me to get involved in another campaign. And then I ended up in the Labour Party. And it took me three selections before I made it on the Council.

But I just sort of – stopped having the time to drink.

Being political – being a political person – saved me.

I don't know why – it suited me. I felt like I was doing good. I guess.

JULIE *says nothing.* MARK *looks at her.*

You're not saying anything about that?

JULIE. No.

MARK. Because it sounded conceited?

JULIE. I don't know.

Maybe... things shouldn't be about what they –

Maybe things shouldn't be about what they do for you.

MARK. No, no – you're wrong – doing it – becoming this –
has changed everything about how I see the world. And by
being – who I am – I've been able to be clearer about what
this Council needs. And I'm proud of myself. And I should
be proud of myself. And I'm proud of you. I'm proud of all
of us.

JULIE. Okay.

She smiles. MARK *looks at her again. He smiles too. There's
a moment's pure silence.*

MARK. Are we together now?

She thinks.

JULIE. Okay.

MARK. You sure?

JULIE. Yeah.

MARK. Why did you take so long to be sure?

JULIE. I thought I could do better.

I was wrong.

MARK. Okay. So I won you. That's what happened. I destroyed
the Council and won you.

JULIE. We haven't destroyed the Council...

MARK. Of course we have.

It's the editorial in the *Guardian* I will particularly remember
– saying that us accusing others of irresponsibility was rich.
That the moral high ground belongs to those who hadn't
previously spent weeks scrabbling around justifying cutting
support for the disabled.

JULIE. Maybe stop googling it. We made the right judgement for the right reasons. We just had to go through a process first. People will see.

MARK. Maybe they won't – not immediately – but eventually – they might. And that's okay. Because we did the right thing. I'm proud of us.

JULIE. And if you say so often enough you might possibly believe it.

MARK. I do believe it.

JULIE *softly kisses* MARK *on the top of the head*.

JULIE. You've got to go.

MARK. I know.

He stands and makes to leave.

JULIE. Mark…

He turns.

You didn't win me. I'm not a fish at the fair. And I'm not settling for anything. I'm choosing – that this is what I want. And I want this to work as much as you do.

MARK *smiles*.

MARK. Good.

Scene Four

HILARY*'s flat*.

HILARY. Come through…

MARK. Is this where you live?

HILARY. Tea? Milk? Sugar?

MARK. Milk. Two sugars. Brown sugar if you have it.

HILARY. I have.

    Would you like a biscuit?

    I only have Rich Tea…

    But they seem to be okay. They seem to be received okay by most people.

    I don't like biscuits.

MARK. Hilary. You live here?

Beat.

HILARY. When I made the decision to go full time on the Council, it required me to downsize. I did so gladly. I live very simply.

MARK. Council flats are nicer than this place.

HILARY. And cheaper. But I decided it would be inappropriate applying for one. It might give the wrong impression.

MARK. You pushed through us reducing our wages and allowances.

    You and me specifically took fifty-per-cent cuts. Year on year.

HILARY. I didn't go into politics to make money, did you?

    This suits me fine. I can afford heat. And I eat fine.

    And I knew you'd be – I knew you had your lecturing.

MARK. Hilary…

HILARY. Not everything is as you expect, is it?

MARK. No. But…

HILARY. Don't pity me, Mark. I don't want to be pitied. Certainly not by you.

    And I invited her here because I didn't want to meet her there.

    Or you.

So don't even – that isn't – she doesn't control everything.

So she has to come here.

MARK. Yeah.

Scene Five

GEORGE*'s house. Top corridor.*

JULIE. Dad? Dad? Are you still in there?

GEORGE. Yes. Still in here and not dead yet. Just shaving.

JULIE. Okay. I quite need a pee.

GEORGE. Retreat. Retreat. Coming out now.

He exits. He's wearing half a head of shaving foam. He looks at her.

Where did you get to last night?

JULIE. Mark's.

GEORGE. Is that so?

JULIE. You told him he needed to be a great man. I said you'd said the same to me more or less every day of my life.

GEORGE. So that put him off the greatness thing?

JULIE. I think I can be happy with him, Dad.

GEORGE. I disagree.

But I admire the conviction.

JULIE. Am I such a disappointment to you?

GEORGE. No. I suspect you're just like me. And that means you're going to make the same mistakes I did.

JULIE. Is that so bad?

GEORGE. Yes.

JULIE. Yes?

The doorbell rings.

Saved by the bell.

JULIE *goes to answer it.*

GEORGE. I thought you needed the toilet –

JULIE. I do.

GEORGE. I thought we were having quite an interesting conversation.

JULIE. I can't not answer the door, Dad. It might be the postman.

GEORGE. Can I finish shaving then?

JULIE. No. Hang on.

She runs down towards the door. GEORGE *follows.*

GEORGE. I'm sorry. I only do honesty, remember.

JULIE. And you think I'm wasting my life just like you did?

GEORGE. And I wish you wouldn't.

JULIE. Yes.

She answers the door.

Oh. Hi.

SARWAN. I wasn't sure where else to go. There seems to be camera crews everywhere.

GEORGE. You're very welcome.

SARWAN. Nice beard. Has she arrived?

JULIE. Not that I've heard.

SARWAN. You read *The Sun* today?

JULIE. No.

SARWAN. It said we were a disgrace to Britain.

JULIE. Yeah?

SARWAN. I bought some Pringles and a family pack of Snickers.

Shall we sit and cower together?

Scene Six

HILARY's *flat*.

HILARY. Well...

They said half past ten. It is now ten past four.

MARK. I imagine...

HILARY. They get to set their own schedules. Yes. I'd imagine that too. But not even an email.

MARK. I know.

HILARY. I imagine they rather like keeping us waiting.

MARK. I imagine they rather like that too.

They sit in silence for a moment more.

You keep glowering at me like you expect me to apologise...

Beat.

HILARY. There is a walk I love to take.

From my flat.

There is something so wonderfully luxurious about walking from your home I think.

A new thing I think that is.

Because in the old days everyone walked from their home.

But today too often some means of transport is involved.

I turn right out of the flats, I walk up the street.

At the top of the road, beside the independent travel agent which always seems to be empty but never goes out of business I turn right.

I walk to the zebra crossing by the roundabout. Too close to the roundabout. I cross it.

I walk up along the A-road. On the pavement beside it, and though this is my least favourite bit of the walk there is something quite fun about having cars race past at sixty miles an hour, and you do feel – there is the feeling that – there is the feeling of danger you get from knowing that at any minute you could step out into the road and feel the car slam into you. Feel the weight of metal jangling through your body.

I cut through the shops to the recreation centre.

I hit my first piece of serious grass. I've been walking you understand for about fifteen to twenty minutes to get to this serious grass.

I step onto the grass.

I walk across the rec centre's land, I cross a fence using the stile and suddenly – everywhere around me is countryside. Everywhere around me – as long as I don't look backwards is pure open green.

And it is – it is the feeling of the grey turning green – it is the feeling of walking into freedom that makes it all so special.

And then you hit a spot and you turn around and you can see the whole town – more or less the whole of the town laid out in front of you.

And it is beautiful.

Because I love this place.

And I am proud to be of this place.

And I don't know – if I didn't have to walk on the A-road, I'm not sure I'd enjoy the countryside so much.

MARK. I do that walk too. But I park at the rec centre. Avoid the first bit.

HILARY. I know I'm not likeable. I've never been likeable.

I've never tried to be likeable.

But I have always tried to do the right thing.

I have always tried to do the right thing.

MARK. Have you?

HILARY. Yes.

MARK. Do you think everyone else hasn't?

HILARY. I think you've been dissuaded by everyone else
telling you what the right thing is.

I think you've confused the right thing with what seems right
and what seems right is never the right thing.

MARK. And I think you've got confused by being in power and
being powerful.

HILARY. We fell into this...

You fell into this hole.

MARK. A man died. We are responsible. We are responsible for
a man's death.

HILARY. So the answer is capitulation?

MARK. No, the answer is to rise above it.

HILARY. Did you really think? Did you really think – you'd
bring people with you...

MARK. No. I thought there was a very strong chance we'd
bring no one at all. That everyone would remain hating us.

But I also thought – I also thought –

It was the good thing to do.

The right thing to do.

That it was time to take a stand.

And fuck the consequences.

She hesitates.

HILARY. So it's a matter of principle?

MARK. Yes.

HILARY. My mother has dementia. She was recently moved into her third care home. Each time she cries, she doesn't know why she cries, but she cries. Many other councils would have put her needs out to tender, they list individual elderly people and invite businesses to submit the lowest bid possible to afford her care.

The doorbell rings.

MARK. I didn't know. About your mother.

HILARY. Oh, everyone has an investment in something. But don't you think... These are people who've given their lives to this country. They deserve better than principle, don't you think? Principle is a privilege we can't afford.

MARK. But isn't that the point? We can't afford principle – so we just get shafted.

The doorbell rings again.

We had a choice, between doing something and doing nothing.

HILARY. And our town had to take the hit on behalf of everyone else, did it?

MARK. Maybe principle is the only way to fight some battles...

HILARY. And maybe it isn't.

MARK. I've spent my entire life thinking – if I hadn't done this or that or the other then none of this would have happened. And it's crushed me.

HILARY. Yes.

MARK. So I've decided to try and think – about it in a new way – that if I hadn't done this or that or the other then none of this would have happened.

HILARY. Didn't you just say the same thing?

MARK. Yes.

HILARY *digests this.*

HILARY. Big risk you've taken really, isn't it?

Big risk with other people's lives.

MARK. We're politicians, Hilary. That's what we do.

There's a hard knock upon the door.

HILARY. I really don't want to answer that door.

Pause.

MARK. Okay.

He stands and walks down the corridor and opens the door.

ALISON. Hello.

MARK. Hello.

They walk through into the kitchen.

HILARY. Hello.

ALISON. Hello.

What a thorough round of hellos.

Always like it when that happens.

Seems so friendly.

You must be Hilary – you must be Mark – and may I say neither of your pictures do you justice.

My name is Alison. I am here on behalf of the UK Parliament.

This is my card.

Just so you know I am who I say I am.

HILARY. You are.

ALISON. First of all, sorry I'm late. Did my assistant ring ahead?

HILARY. No.

ALISON. Well, then that's the first cock-up of the day. We got stuck in at Whitehall.

And then getting out here took longer than I expected.

I thought I was in the wrong place at first. Extraordinary building.

IIILARY. Not that extraordinary.

ALISON. And what an extraordinary lift.

Anyway, I am here because this Council is in default. Is that how you understand the situation too?

HILARY. It is.

MARK. Yes.

ALISON. I want to make clear at this point that I am not of any particular political persuasion. Try saying that when drunk. I am a civil servant, appointed by the incumbent government to assist on matters of local government.

You have – refused – to set a budget.

So now, as laid down in section 114 of the Local Government Act 1988 we're going to work with your Chief Finance Officer – your S151 Officer – in order to make a budget for you.

Is that how you understand the situation too?

HILARY. Yes.

MARK. Yes.

ALISON. So – today – I am going to – this is just a conversation – there is nothing aggressive about it – a conversation about what happens next for this Council.

When you all resign your governance to me. And – with your S151 Officer – my department will work to balance the books. After which time you will resume full control of the tiller.

Is that how you understand the situation too?

HILARY. Can I beg...? Can I please beg? Can I beg you don't – that you try and protect some of what made this town function?

ALISON. That is entirely why I'm here, Hilary.

To make this town functional again.

Scene Seven

Newtown day centre.

GINA. Okay. You'll like this one. What did the rabbit give his girlfriend?

LAURA. I don't know.

GINA. A fourteen-carrot ring.

She does a Bugs Bunny impression with a carrot. LAURA *laughs.*

What do you get when you pour hot water down a rabbit hole?

LAURA. I don't know.

GINA. A hot-cross bunny.

LAURA *laughs.*

LAURA. That one was better.

GINA. Why did the bald man paint bunnies on his head?

LAURA. Are all the jokes about rabbits?

GINA. Because from a distance they looked like hares.

LAURA *doesn't laugh.*

Not so good?

LAURA. I'm going to guess the next one.

GINA. Okay.

Pause.

LAURA. They told me they're shutting the library.

GINA. I heard that too.

LAURA. What will they do with the books?

GINA. I don't know.

LAURA. Can I have some?

GINA. Maybe.

LAURA. Will they shut here too?

GINA. I think it's likely.

LAURA. What will you do?

GINA. Get a new job I think.

LAURA. What will I do?

GINA. I don't know.

LAURA. Okay. Okay.

> *Pause.*

Can you tell another joke about rabbits? One I can guess?

GINA. Why did the carrot cross the road?

LAURA. I can get this. Because…

GINA. You'll get there.

LAURA. Because it wanted – something about rabbits.

GINA. Yes. Something about rabbits.

LAURA. Okay.

> Give me time. I'll get there.

> *She smiles up at* GINA. *Who smiles back.*

Scene Eight

Council chambers. Committee room.

HILARY. So here they are – hot off the press.

The documents get passed around the room.

JULIE. They're just – giving them to us?

SARWAN. I thought we'd have to steal them too.

HILARY. But they're not for us to discuss.

This is what's happening.

They're letting us know what's happening.

SARWAN. Shall we read them out or...?

HILARY. We're above reading age.

We'll just read ourselves, shall we?

They read through, and we watch, and this takes a little bit of time.

This takes quite a lot of time.

This takes a huge amount of time.

And we just watch their faces.

SARWAN *sits up first. He looks around the faces.*

SARWAN. So that's...

JULIE. Yes.

HILARY. Five Sure Start Centres. Six homes for the elderly. And they seem to be contracting out everything.

LATA. Gina's day centre. Closed. Your mum's home. Closed.

JULIE. But this seems...

HILARY. It does, doesn't it?

LATA. They're anticipating next year's cuts, I'm guessing.

SARWAN. No. They're making an example of us.

MARK. Yes.

Yes. They are.

HILARY. We've made our statement and so have they.

And now – and now –

This is what it feels like.

This is what it feels like when you... step out of line.

JULIE. Or this is what it feels like when everything changes...

HILARY *looks at* JULIE *and smiles kindly.*

HILARY. I hope you're right, Julie.

MARK. Maybe we've done a great thing.

Maybe we've been fools.

History will judge.

HILARY. Yes. History...

Or maybe the *Guardian*.

Or maybe – Twitter.

JULIE. And – in the meantime – what do we do?

HILARY. We get on with being a Council again.

ACT FIVE

Scene One

Victoria Park. A bench.

GEORGE. Do you mind if I sit here?

JAKE. No.

GEORGE. It's the only spot free. Too nice a day. Always brings
out the... and benches don't reward loyalty. Even though I'm
out here every day whatever the weather.

JAKE. Yeah.

GEORGE. And I can't sit on the grass, terrible knees.

JAKE. It's okay. You can sit where you like.

GEORGE. Shouldn't you be gallivanting around with your
friends?

JAKE *looks at* GEORGE.

JAKE. Shouldn't you...

GEORGE. Quite right.

Quite right.

That deserved that response.

And actually I'm running from friends – well, my daughter's
friends who are also sort of my friends –

What are you reading?

JAKE. *Great Expectations*.

GEORGE. Ah. Now that's... Where are you?

JAKE. Almost at the end. Ten pages from the end.

GEORGE. Do you like it?

JAKE. Yeah. Yeah. Actually. It's really good.

GEORGE. Are you reading it for school?

JAKE. No. Just me. Have you read it?

GEORGE. Yes. Yes. I thought it was really good too. Quite special. Bit didactic on the notion of class differences but very good.

JAKE. Why's it didactic?

GEORGE. It sort of suggests working-class people are salt of the earth, upper-class people are venal.

JAKE. No. It doesn't. Mrs Joe is a bitch.

GEORGE *thinks and then smiles.*

GEORGE. Yes. She is. You're entirely right.

Maybe it's more sophisticated than I thought.

Big reader?

JAKE. I try to be.

GEORGE. Good. Yes. Me too. Nice to be somewhere else, isn't it?

JAKE. Yeah.

Pause.

GEORGE. What do you think the book is trying to say?

JAKE. We don't have to talk.

GEORGE. No. Of course not. Much apologies. Who wants a – who wants an old man talking to them.

Pause. JAKE*S reopens his book. He starts to read. Then he shuts it again.*

JAKE. Go on then. You've got me interested.

What do you think it's about?

GEORGE. *Great Expectations?*

JAKE. Yeah.

GEORGE. I think it's about – the future. I think it's about how the future makes a fool out of you.

JAKE. Yeah. It's not.

GEORGE. You did that clever trick of making me speak first – are you going to make me feel ignorant now?

JAKE. No. Just tell you what I think. I think it's about how shit it is trying to be like everyone else. And I think it's about trying – I think it's about how trying is good. But hard. I actually think it's quite optimistic. I mean, everyone are utter wankers in it but I still think Pip is better off – you know – for having tried. I reckon he'll work out okay in the end. He might even be happy.

Pause. GEORGE *smiles.*

GEORGE. Would you like some marijuana?

JAKE. Sorry?

GEORGE. I have some medical marijuana – that I smoke – would you like to share it with me? It feels rude to smoke it alone.

JAKE. You're offering me weed?

GEORGE. Medical weed makes it sound less of a felony.

JAKE. You realise this is a public park?

GEORGE. I've already rolled it. I like to smoke it outside so my daughter can't smell it on the curtains…

JAKE. Right.

GEORGE. And as for the public… smoking it in public…

I find people are generally quite liberal when it comes to marijuana. I've never once had anyone come over and complain.

JAKE. Okay.

GEORGE. Okay you will?

JAKE. Yes.

GEORGE. Great.

He takes out a tin and removes a joint.

Would you like to go first or second?

JAKE. First.

GEORGE. Starting it off requires a little persistence but I'm sure you have it in you.

JAKE. Right.

What's wrong with you?

GEORGE. What on earth do you mean?

JAKE. You said it's medical – what's wrong with you?

GEORGE. I'm old.

JAKE. It's prescribed because you're old?

GEORGE. It's not prescribed, child. I'm self-medicating. Because I've had a hard life but I look at you and know you'll never have it as good as I did.

JAKE. Good to know.

GEORGE. Marijuana makes – for me, marijuana makes the world nicer. And maybe it'll do the same for you.

I think you could do with a happier world.

JAKE. Okay. I get it.

You're smoking because you're a fuck-up?

GEORGE *smiles.*

GEORGE. Yes. Yes. That's it.

I'm smoking because I am proud fucking fuck-up.

He looks at JAKE.

JAKE. It is possible though, just so you know, it's possible I will have a better life than you. It's possible the world will be better. More equal. Better. Just so you know.

GEORGE *digests that with a smile.*

GEORGE. If you try?

JAKE. Exactly.

GEORGE. And will you try?

JAKE *considers*.

JAKE. You've got to, right? I mean, it's sort of pointless, isn't it? Not trying?

I mean, the world's sort of pointless – if you don't try.

GEORGE. Yes. Yes. It probably is.

Pause. GEORGE *turns thoughts over in his head. He smiles*.

You know what, kid? You've almost cheered me up.

Now can you light my joint please? I'm getting impatient.

Scene Two

LATA *looks forward*.

LATA. How can I help?

SARWAN *takes a breath and then looks forward*.

SARWAN. How can I help?

JULIE *looks at* SARWAN *and then looks forward*.

JULIE. How can I help?

HILARY. How can I help?

MARK. How can I help?

GEOFF. Well, actually…

I'm here because…

My allotment charges have gone up. £35 a year. And I don't think that's fair.

Beat.

SARWAN. Great. Let's see what we can do.

The End.

A Nick Hern Book

Hope first published as a paperback original in Great Britain in 2014 by Nick Hern Books Limited, The Glasshouse, 49a Goldhawk Road, London W12 8QP, in association with the Royal Court Theatre

Cover photo by Leandro Farina

Designed and typeset by Nick Hern Books, London
Printed in Great Britain by CPI Group (UK) Ltd

A CIP catalogue record for this book is available from the British Library

ISBN   978 1 84842 447 0